W9-CYW-994

Caste in Contemporary India: Beyond Organic Solidarity

Caste in Contemporary India: Beyond Organic Solidarity

Pauline Kolenda
University of Houston

WAVELAND
PRESS, INC.
Prospect Heights, Illinois

For information about this book, write or call:
Waveland Press, Inc.
P.O. Box 400
Prospect Heights, Illinois 60070
(708) 634-0081

Cover: Eating is not a commensal activity in traditional India. The man of the house may eat alone, even outside the house, rather than the entire family eating together. The ease with which food is polluted by other people probably accounts for isolated eating. *[Photo by Pauline Kolenda]*

Preface

The popular Western response to Indian caste has often been one of shock. The caste system has appeared to be one in which an individual inherits an occupation, in which occupations are ranked, and in which an individual's worth or worthlessness is ordained by birth. Actually, the possibility of social mobility through modern Western-style education and occupational advancement came to India quite some time ago, even if it did so minimally at first. Inheritance of caste occupation has been disappearing as a feature of caste membership for the past century with mixed results; these are discussed in this book.

My primary objective in writing *Caste in Contemporary India* was to emphasize the idea that the endogamous birth-descent group, the *jāti*—the basic unit of the caste system—is essentially a large-scale kin group. Despite the gradual demise of the occupational aspect of the caste system (a demise now taking place at a more rapid tempo), the solidarity of the *jāti* is intact. Thus India presents the sociological possibility of becoming a modern society that yet retains what Ibn Khaldūn called *asabiyah*, the tribal spirit, a morale which Khaldūn believed was inevitably lost with the advance of civilization. It is, of course, a possibility that such group solidarities may be supportive for individuals yet dangerous to a modern democracy. We have yet to see whether castes will fuse into contending power blocks splitting the body politic and perpetuating "casteism."

It is evident from the material discussed in this book that the shape of India emerging will be different from the shape of modern Western societies. Caste in its new transformations will be an important contributing factor in determining that shape.

About the Author

Pauline Kolenda received her B.A. from Wellesley College and her Ph.D. from Cornell University. She is presently Professor of Anthropology at the University of Houston. She has served on the Board of Directors of the Association for Asian Studies and as president of the Southwest Conference on Asian Studies. She has done many stints of fieldwork in India, working in four different states: Uttar Pradesh, Rajasthan, Maharashtra, and Tamilnadu. Most of her writings concern caste, family, and religion in Indian culture, although she has also written on the ballet company (with Sondra Forsyth) and on ethnic prejudice in the United States. Many of her papers appear in a collection, Caste, Cult and Hierarchy (New Delhi: Folklore Institute, Manohar Book Service, 1981).

Contents

Acknowledgments

Such a summary on caste in contemporary India as this one owes most to all the scholars whose work I have drawn upon. This includes the general social structural point of view taken, which comes out of recent social anthropology, and the many studies by anthropologists, political scientists, historians, archeologists, sociologists, and journalists. Their names appear in the text itself. I fully realize that many excellent studies have been overlooked; I plead normal human frailty. And, of course, we all owe, individuably and collectively, our thanks to the thousands of gracious Indians who cooperated in these myriad studies.

I owe thanks to Helena Kolenda for making the index, to Victor Mote for making the maps, to Hyla Converse, Marvin Davis, McKim Marriott, and Kant Patel who read portions of the manuscript and gave me advice, to Konstantin Kolenda who read it all, to everyone at The Benjamin/Cummings Publishing Company who gave long hours and effort to get it into readable and photo-ready form, to Jo Monaghan and Suzanne Terrell who typed drafts of it, to Ward Goodenough, Gerald Batte, Konstantin Kolenda, and Robert Hardgrave for encouragement.

Introduction

> Caste cannot be abolished in India, and to attempt it would be one of the most hazardous operations that was ever performed in a political body. As a religious institution caste will die; as a social institution, it will live and improve.
>
> (Max Muller 1869: 353)

> . . . one school said that modernization of these societies is impossible because of the strength of their traditional social institutions and beliefs; the other held that modernization is possible provided that the traditional system is eliminated or transformed into a modern system of nuclear families, social classes, free markets, rational-bureaucratic organizations, and an achievement-oriented scientific world view.
>
> Since the end of the Second World War, and the coming of independence and partition of the Indian subcontinent, a third school of scholarly opinion has developed on this issue of modernization. . . . this school asks, not *whether* modernization is possible in South Asia, but rather *how* it takes place.
>
> (Singer 1973: 2)

"Is there *still* a caste system in India?"

It is often assumed that the caste system in South Asia has faded away. Yet it is indeed unlikely that a

1

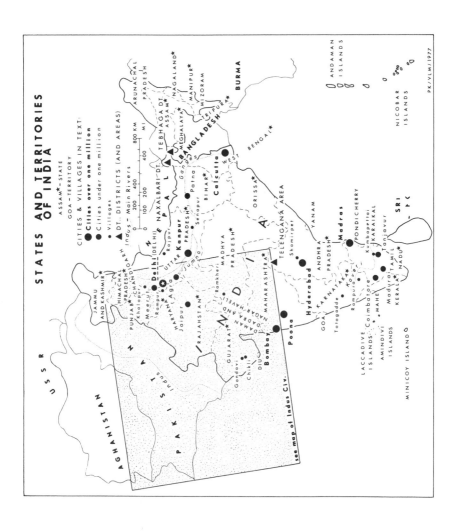

STATES AND TERRITORIES OF INDIA

social structure organizing the political, economic, and ritual life of a people for over one thousand years could be totally expunged within a few decades. Social scientists who have worked recently in the countries of South Asia all report that the caste system is alive. Whether it is both alive *and well* is one of the questions addressed in this book.

Western observers have emphasized the inequities and consequent injustices of the system. "The Hindu social order," said the American sociologist, Kingsley Davis, "is the most thoroughgoing attempt known in human history to introduce absolute inequality as the guiding principle in social relations." (Davis 1951: 170) More recently, the anthropologist Gerald Berreman has spoken out against the "sentence" which birth deals out to the member of a caste "for life." For the lower-caste person, that sentence is a life of disprivileges of all sorts. (Berreman 1972a) The French social anthropologist, Louis Dumont, accuses such critics of being sociocentric—perceiving and judging from the vantage point of one's own society. Dumont argues that, in contrast to the competitive Western system which emphasizes individual ambition, the caste system involves a "holism," an orientation toward the welfare of all. Certainly all castes do not receive equal rewards; but this, he explains, is because all do not contribute equally, as judged by the underlying values of the caste system. Thus, Dumont argues that although all castes are not equally rewarded, all are integrated into the system. By Hindu ideals, all are cared for; the system exists for the benefit of all (Dumont 1970: 107).

Whether one accepts Dumont's evaluation of Westerners as sociocentric or ethnocentric, we can at least identify the American values that run counter to the caste system: a belief in equal opportunities for all in education and occupation, "success" and upward mobility as possibilities for all, and an emphasis upon individual fulfillment. These values are related to an expanding economy in a rich natural environment, the rapid technological-economic change we call the industrial revolution, and the absence in America of feudal social structure (Riesman 1950; Williams 1951; Whyte 1956; Moore 1966).

The caste system is related to a different economic and political context—a stagnant paleotechnic agrarian economy supporting some craftsmen, priests and religious mendicants, a monarch, his bureaucracy, and an army in a chronically unstable political condition. To find parallels with such a society in the West, one draws upon concepts from the Middle Ages—feudalism, the manor, *noblesse oblige*, estates, fealty to one's lord, subordination to one's "betters," the conception of society as an organism in which each social segment contributed its function, the uneasy balance between church and state, the peasantry protected in the lord's fortress, the Hundred Years' Wars.

If we agree that the Indian caste system is a pre-industrial institution, one developed before the industrial revolution, we may then ask if it is an obstacle to industrial revolution—or to what social scientists commonly call "modernization." Max Weber's *The Religion of India*, originally published in 1921, was a particularly scholarly and persuasive argument that Hinduism and the caste system—supported by Hindu beliefs in rebirth, retribution, and reward for meritorious and sinful behavior—would function as obstacles to modern capitalism and industry. A number of contemporary scholars, whether directly influenced by Weber or not, have held his opinion. Most influential currently is the Swedish economist, Gunnar Myrdal, who sees the caste system as an obstacle to economic and political modernization (Myrdal 1972: 80, 147, 177). In contrast, others have found the caste system to be flexible and adaptive, most notably, the anthropologist, Milton Singer (Singer 1972, 1973), and the historical sociologist, Barrington Moore, Jr. (Moore 1966: 334).

In this book both the constancies and the adaptations of the Indian caste system will be discussed. The constant feature in caste is its kinship or descent-group structure. On the other hand, a key feature which adapts or is, in some instances, in decline is occupational specialization. The caste *system* represented by a set of interdependent artisans or servants is in decline. Showing signs of decline also is the system of purity and pollution which ranked castes relative to each other, and kept them separate from one another. So the traditional caste system as a set of occupationally-specialized, interdependent castes, ranked by purity and pollution customs, shows signs of disappearing. Whether there will be a new integration into a new caste system is a key question. Evidence suggests that a new system would have a competitive solidarity, as fused combinations of castes compete with one another. This is in contrast to the cooperative but hierarchical organic solidarity of the traditional system.

In this book, caste is first considered as a system of descent-groups—a system which can be understood by means of the same concepts social anthropologists have used to understand tribal peoples elsewhere. Then the traditional caste system is analyzed, the evidence for its decline discussed, and the characteristics of the emerging new caste system examined. The hierarchical structure of caste and its inequities are evident in the description of the traditional system. It is then important to consider whether such inequities and hierarchical ordering will persist and be injected into a new caste system.

Chapter 1

Castes as Descent-Groups

The most persistent feature of Indian society is its organization into micro-communities which are large-scale descent-groups. One form of this organization is *castes*. There are large-scale descent-groups other than castes. Before castes, and co-existing today with castes, are tribes; and after castes have been released from caste *systems*, in which each caste takes a specialized role in a ritualized division of labor, there are and will be large-scale descent-groups which might be called *kin-communities*.

The organization of a national population into thousands of micro-communities may account in considerable measure for the stability of India despite poverty, governmental ineffectiveness, and other problems. Such an organization shapes, and is likely to continue to shape, a process of modernization that is significantly different from that with which we are familiar in the West.

INDIAN DESCENT-GROUPS AND WESTERN KINSHIP

The persistence of caste in India, even among educated and modernized Indians, is due to a kind of micro-community organization that the West does not have. Certainly, this kind of kinship structuring of Indian castes does not characterize racial groups in the United States. In fact, the kinship organization of

6

Indian castes distinguishes them from "castes" in the United States and possibly elsewhere. (For comparisons between caste in India and in the United States, see Berreman 1966, 1967b, 1973; Harper 1968b; Pitt-Rivers 1971; Dumont 1970: 239-258). The micro-community organization of Indian castes is more characteristic of *tribes* elsewhere than it is of either classes or racial segments in modern Western society. (See Hutton 1963; Karve 1968; Sahlins 1968).

Referring to the Indian descent-groups as "large" implies a comparison. An Indian caste is large as compared to the kinship network of one's kindred or "relatives" in Western society. For a child in the West the kinship group is a modified extended family composed of perhaps two sets of grandparents, the siblings of one's parents plus their spouses and children, plus one's own siblings—a set numbering perhaps fifty to two hundred persons (Schneider and Cottrell 1975: 31). An Indian caste may include thousands or even tens of thousands. If, on the other hand, one were to compare the caste in size with a national political party, it would seem to be small. Throughout this study, the former comparison with family kinship groups is used. Hence the caste is considered a large-scale descent-group.

Western society is not organized by descent-groups. Both in the pre-modern and modern West, there has been a strong focus upon the nuclear family. The kindred, the set of kin traced through both parents, who were obligated to an individual, might or might not be strongly bound to that person. Family kinship networks were *not* bounded corporate descent-groups. Robert Anderson suggests that "the Seignorial system" during the feudal period in Europe disrupted extended kinship networks. The lord controlled peasant marriages, inheritance, and succession, and families on one manor were cut off from those on another. As a result, the nuclear family on a small plot of land was obligated to, and depended upon their lord rather than upon ties of lineage, clan, or kindred (Anderson 1971: 145). The northern European emphasis upon the nuclear family is one of several centuries standing (Arensberg 1960; Laslett 1965, 1972).

Talcott Parsons has referred to the American reckoning of kin as *multilineal*, all lines of descent being

equally important or equally unimportant because the
American system puts major emphasis upon the nuclear
family (isolated from a descent group) (Parsons 1943).
As Radcliffe-Brown pointed out, the use of a *unilineal*
descent principle, focusing upon only one line out of
several lines of ancestry, makes possible the recogni-
tion of a more farflung array of kin than does an equal
emphasis upon two or more lines of descent. An emphasis on unilineal descent facilitates the organization
of corporate groups that endure beyond the life of an
individual or family (Radcliffe-Brown 1950: 42).

In India, descent-groups are unilineal—usually
patrilineal, but in some parts, the Southwest and
Northeast, they are matrilineal. Unlike the Chinese,
Indians do not put much emphasis upon maintaining
genealogies (Fried 1957: 16), except among some past
or would-be ruling lines, notably the Rajputs of northern and central India. However, sets of patrilineages
form clans or sibs which, in turn, form endogamous
units called *jātis*. Under this organization, a bridegroom receives a bride from a near or distant segment
of a descent-group, although the families involved in
the alliance may or may not be able to trace the actual
lineage distance of the individuals involved.

Thus, the basic building block of Indian society
has been the large-scale descent-group, structured by a
unilineal principle, composed of a hierarchy of increasingly inclusive segments. At some levels the segments may be exogamous, at some levels endogamous. The
whole descent-group composes a tribe, *jāti*, or kin-
community. The minimal segments of the descent-group
typically form residential units in hamlet, village,
town, or city. Thus localized units of the descent-
group are dispersed over a region or regions.

TRIBE, CASTE, AND KIN-COMMUNITY

In pre-modern society, a tribe, as an ideal type at
least, is the large-scale descent-group subsisting in
isolation. The tribe may be composed of pastoralists,
agriculturalists, artisans, or hunters. It has its own
culture or sub-culture. It is a group *not* integrated
with others in a caste system.

The *caste* is the descent-group with a special role
by which it is integrated into a traditional local or
regional system of inter-dependence and interchange
with other groups—a caste *system*. The caste may or may
not have a distinctive sub-culture.
Finally, the *kin-community* is defined as the
large-scale descent-group *released* from a system of
caste interdependence. The kin-community is adapted
to the institutions of the modern occupational, political, and educational environment. It operates for the
welfare of its members, on whose behalf it functions as
a kindred, a resource network, a pressure group, a voluntary organization, or an ethnic group.
The three social types—the tribe, the caste, and
the kin-community—can be seen as transformations of a
single underlying descent-group structure. It is
tempting to order these three types chronologically and
to say that the tribe existed first. Then, perhaps,
the tribe became a caste as Hindu village life was established. Lastly, one could hypothesize the development of the kin-community about 1820, when modernization and its concomitants—such as population pressure,
land shortages, and cash-cropping—increasingly undermined the traditional caste system with the correspond-
ing emergence of new adaptations of the basic structure.
In fact, all three types of social unit exist in
India today. About 45 million people are listed by the
Census of India of 1971 as tribals (Gough 1974: 1407).
However, most of India's 580 million people continue to
live in rural areas, and most still participate in some
way in a traditional local caste system. Yet, as will
be discussed, increasing numbers of people are involun-
tarily losing their place in the traditional system.
At the same time, a gradually increasing number of people are being integrated occupationally into a largely
caste-free modern occupational structure involving government, businesses, factories, schools, colleges, and
services of various kinds.
Not only do all three social types coexist in
India, but they may coexist in one micro-community like
that of the Santals. Labeled by the government as
tribals, and numbering about 3 million people, they
include in their midst social units definable as
tribes, castes, and kin-communities (Orans 1965).

This view of the caste system, with an emphasis on lineage structure, is influenced by the social anthropological work of such scholars as Meyer Fortes (1945, 1945a, 1969), E. E. Pritchard (1940), Radcliffe-Brown (1935, 1941, 1950), and Marshall Sahlins (1968). Such an emphasis was transferred to an analysis of Indian caste most notably by John Hitchcock (1956), Adrian Mayer (1958, 1960), M. N. Srinivas (1959, 1962, 1969), F. G. Bailey, (1957, 1960, 1963), Louis Dumont (1970), Robert Hardgrave (1968), and Brenda Beck (1972).

Jāti and Caste. To suggest that it is the descent-group which is the constant in Indian society is not to do injustice to the Indian native view. English-speaking Indians frequently refer to their caste as their "community." The word $j\bar{a}ti$, most often used as the Hindi word for caste, has many meanings. Bhargava's Standard Hindi-English Dictionary translates $j\bar{a}ti$ as "birth, life, race, sex, lineage, parentage, state, tribe, caste, set, quality, genus, species, nature, family, sort, kind, name, order, nation, section, peoples, clan, community, breed." Our anthropological term, descent-group, also suggests that it is a group into which one is born, in which one has parents, as well as lineal ancestors. The term $j\bar{a}ti$ could include all three of the transformations suggested—tribe, caste, and kin-community.

The Indian social anthropologist, André Béteille, says that in his experience the word jati may be used to refer to linguistic, regional, and religious categories of persons. Even when the term jati is used in a caste context, Béteille states, it may refer to a sub-caste, caste, caste category, or to a caste association—all of which will be discussed (Béteille 1969: 45-49, 55, 146). In this book the Hindi word $j\bar{a}ti$ will be used synonymously with the anthropological term sub-$caste$ to mean an endogamous large-scale descent-group, a connubium. Mandelbaum (1970) uses it similarly. (See Marriott and Inden, 1972.)

The English word "caste" is a translation of the Portuguese $casta$, a word used by Portuguese in India to describe the jati-system. (The Portuguese colonized parts of India beginning late in the fifteenth century; officially they lost their last colonies there in 1975.) The connotation or meaning of the Portuguese casta is close to that of the Hindi word, jati. Both mean species, breed, race, or lineage. Also, until the nineteenth century, the words casta and caste were used to refer to both tribes and castes in India (Pitt-Rivers 1971: 234). So *casta* could also apply to tribe, caste, and kin-community. In this book, however, the term caste will be used to refer to a set of *jatis* sharing the same name, occupation, and ethnic history.

India can be compared with Europe in cultural and linguistic diversity. There are important regional differences in caste, but it is useful to describe a model or ideal type of *a caste*.

A Model Caste. Think of the 620 million people of India divided into thousands of mutually exclusive micro-communities, each person belonging to only one. The quality of relationships between the members within each is highly personal and almost entirely face-to-face. Each micro-community, in fact, is a kind of oversized kinship group whose members are related either closely or distantly by blood or marriage, so that members think of each other as kinsmen.

Rules for behavior within the micro-community are well-defined, agreed upon, and rather consistently sanctioned. There are councils at various levels within the community for enforcement of rules, for meting out justice in disputes, and for social planning. Social control of members is usually strong and effective. Since each micro-community usually has its own special skill or work, and its own gods, the micro-community is more than a kinship group and a political constituency. It is also a work group, even sometimes a trade union, and a religious congregation. Thus, the micro-community is multiplex, fulfilling many functions for its members. Such a community is intensely interested in each of its members. By some standards this results in a lack of personal privacy or in limiting the scope for individual initiative and expression. However, intense group interest may also mean a life free from the *anomie* or feeling of meaninglessness which Émile Durkheim (1897) saw as a common occurrence for the modern individual when he or she lacks guiding norms or group membership. As Sir Henry Maine saw long ago, castes have a "solidity . . . which has no counterpart in the Western world" (Maine 1895: 219).

If members live entirely within the micro-community, we call that community a tribe. If, however, each community is related to other micro-communities in a sector of inter-dependent relationships—the grouping is called a caste, although it may still remain "tribe-like."
There are reasons for emphasizing the tribal quality of caste life. First, many castes existing at present go back to a tribal origin, such as the pastoral Ahirs and Gujars. Secondly, as previously stated, the native Indian term for caste (jati) also covers tribe. Thirdly, the institutions within a caste are similar to those within a tribe and can be well understood in terms of the concepts which anthropologists have developed for describing tribes in various other parts of the world.

FROM TRIBE TO CASTE

There are about 45 million tribal peoples in India today (Gough 1974: 1407). They are located in the mountains and desert across Central India, South India, and the Northeast. They tend to dwell in geographically marginal refuge areas—reflecting their historical escape from the agents of Hindu culture. There are no *pure* tribes today in the sense of homogeneous, egalitarian, isolated, self-sufficient total societies within which all aspects of life are carried on. Although there are still vast differences among Indian tribes in the degree of their integration into Hindu village caste life, all are now integrated into either caste-like relations with other social segments, or into modern cash markets or employment (Bose 1971: 15, 20, 26-28, 37). Tribals are no longer culturally distinctive from Hindu peasants. Tribals today usually identify themselves as Hindu (although many in the Northeast are Christians).
It is useful to use a caste-tribe continuum in comparing tribal and peasant peoples (see L. P. Vidyarthi 1972; Ram P. Srivastava 1966; C. von Fürer-Haimendorf 1967; Nirmal Kumar Bose 1971; Kushwant Singh 1965; Frederick Bailey 1960). In looking at the social evolutionary process, from tribe to caste, more care-

fully, it is useful to follow Surajit Sinha in specifying a number of different processes involved. Since change does not take place in every area at the same rate, a single tribe might be assigned different places along each of a number of sub-continua (Sinha 1965: 78).
Some of these processes or sub-continua would be cultural; some would be social. Cultural processes might include Hinduization—the acceptance of Hindu gods, religious concepts, rituals, and priests. Another cultural process would have to do with acceptance of the Hindu Pollution Concept which involves the belief that castes differ in their inherent quality of purity or pollution. Some tribals have accepted such beliefs (Bailey 1960: 175).
A social sub-process or sub-dimension would concern the degree to which a group was interdependent with other groups. Bailey, for example, in his study of the Kond tribals of Orissa, distinguishes these tribals from the Oriya Hindu peasants by showing that Konds remained independent politically even while under Oriya rule. The tribal Konds are rather like the dominant caste among the Hindu peasant Oriyas, in that both have control over the agriculturally-productive land and have lower castes dependent upon them. However, the Konds compose a much higher proportion of the population (80 percent) of the locality they dominate, as compared to the locality the Oriya Warrior caste dominates (19 percent). Castes subordinate to both are rather like conquered peoples in their dependency (Bailey 1960: 265; 1957: 49).
Bailey's tribe-caste continuum refers to this relationship of political dependence. He describes it as follows:

> . . . at one end . . . is a society whose political system is entirely of the segmentary egalitarian type, and which contains no dependents whatsoever; and at the other end of which is a society in which segmentary political relations exist only between a very small proportion of the total society, and most people act in the system in the role of dependents. . . . Just at what point on the continuum tribe ceases and caste begins it is impossible to say . . . (Bailey 1960: 264-265).

SEGMENTATION WITHIN THE MICRO-COMMUNITY

Even when, on a tribe-caste continuum, the tribes have
clearly become castes—the castes will differ in their
places along both the cultural and social sub-continua.
They will differ in degree of commitment to orthodox
Hindu values, in the richness and uniqueness of their
sub-cultural life, and in the importance of their roles
in the religio-economic system of ritual redistribution
and exchange—what has been called the Hindu *jajmāni*
system. (The client for whom an artisan or servant
works is a *jajmān*. From the *jajmān*, the system takes
its name, the jajmani system (Wiser 1936). See page
46: The Hindu Jajmani System.)
    Like descent-groups in other parts of the world,
both tribes and castes in India are polysegmental, each
segment characterized by its own special functions.
The segment at each higher level in a hierarchy includes those at a lower level. So a domestic family
combines with others to form a lineage, usually a
patrilineage of rather shallow depth—that is, one of
seldom more than the seven generations that are within
the cognizance of living members. A large number of
such lineages belong to a clan or sib, a unilineal
descent group in which actual descent cannot be traced;
but descent is believed to have occurred from some common ancestor. Members of a sib are *putative* descendants of a common ancestor. One calls members of one's
own sib by kin terms—they are fathers, mothers, brothers, or sisters, and so on—but this is a matter of
courtesy rather than of exact relationship. Often
called a *gotra*, the clan or sib is usually exogamous.
The word, *gotra*, is derived from a Sanskrit word meaning cattleshed. Gotras first appeared historically
among the ancient Brahman priests and referred to fol-
lowers of the same ancient seer (Basham 1954: 148-149).
The names of the Brahman gotras have been borrowed and
used by many other castes as have the gotras of the
Rajputs, a large cluster of warriors and rulers in
northern India. In other cases, gotra names often indicate a region or city, possibly once the places of
origin of their members.

The Gōtra. The gotra is a dispersed sib or clan. Its
various lineage segments are located in many different
localities. On the other hand, within a locality such
as in a jati hamlet or ward, the lineage of one sib may
alone or with lineages belonging to other sibs form the
group of cooperation in life-cycle and other rituals.
Its adult males may form a self-governing council,
possibly with an hereditary head. This jati colony
usually provides some service or product to other
castes within the multi-caste village or locality—
receiving reciprocal services and products in exchange.

A number of gotras, as well as a number of jati
colonies, form a *sub-caste* or entire jati, the endogamous unit. (See Figure 1.1 on page 16.) Sometimes
lineages or clans are ranked within a sub-caste; sometimes sub-castes are ranked within a caste. In Northern India, clans may be ranked, as among the Rajputs
and Marathas. In South India, sub-castes are sometimes
ranked, as among the Tamil Brahmans.

Similar to gotras are surnames in Maharashtra, and
house names in Andhra Pradesh. Such dispersed sibs are
usually exogamous. Sometimes relationships between a
pair of sibs may be conceptualized as patrilineal relations. There may be "brother" gotras or "brother"
house-names between which marriages are prohibited. It
is more usual, however, for marriages to take place *between* these exogamous sibs. Indeed, regulation of marriage seems to be the only function of most such sibs.

Maureen Patterson (1968) described the caste
structure of the Chitpavan Brahmans of Maharashtra as
fourteen exogamous patrilineal sibs called gotras.
(See Figure 1.2, page 17.) Thirteen of these gotras
were grouped into six *gatas* or *ganas*, five of two
gotras each, and one of three gotras. Persons belonging to gotras within the same gata cannot marry. Marriages thus are normally both inter-gotra and inter-
gata except for the fourteenth gotra which can marry
into any of the other gotras. Each Chitpavan gotra is
composed of 300 or more patrilineages called *kulas*.
These, in turn, are divided into a dozen to one hundred
lineage segments, each usually associated with a town
or village (Patterson 1968: 407-409).

Figure 1.1

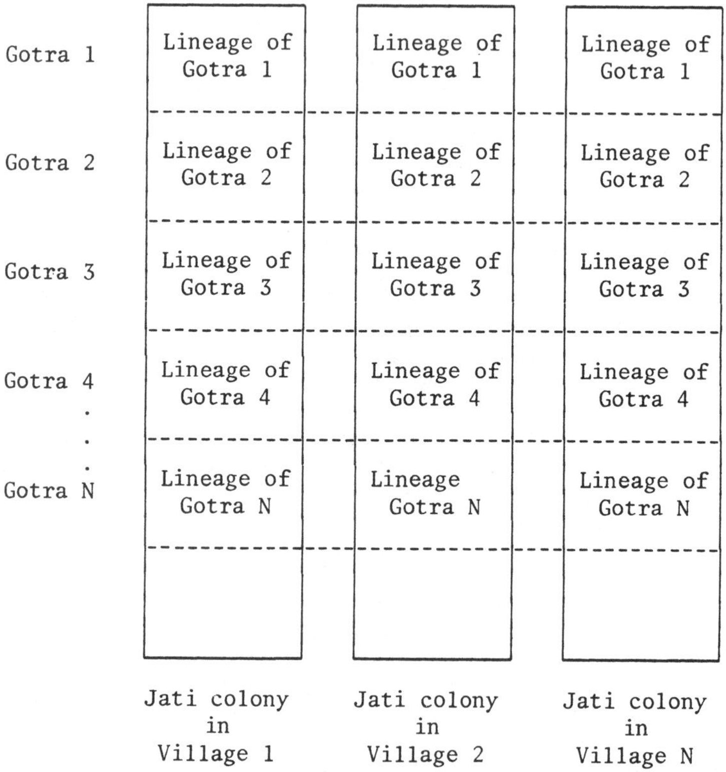

	Jati colony in Village 1	Jati colony in Village 2	Jati colony in Village N
Gotra 1	Lineage of Gotra 1	Lineage of Gotra 1	Lineage of Gotra 1
Gotra 2	Lineage of Gotra 2	Lineage of Gotra 2	Lineage of Gotra 2
Gotra 3	Lineage of Gotra 3	Lineage of Gotra 3	Lineage of Gotra 3
Gotra 4 . . .	Lineage of Gotra 4	Lineage of Gotra 4	Lineage of Gotra 4
Gotra N	Lineage of Gotra N	Lineage Gotra N	Lineage of Gotra N

A number of gotras as well as a number of jati colonies form a sub-caste or entire jati, the endogamous unit.

Figure 1.2

Structure of the Chitpavan Brahman Caste of Maharashtra
(derived from Patterson 1968: 407-409)

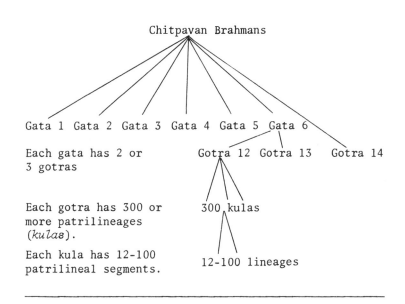

Chitpavan Brahmans

Gata 1 Gata 2 Gata 3 Gata 4 Gata 5 Gata 6

Each gata has 2 or
3 gotras

Gotra 12 Gotra 13   Gotra 14

Each gotra has 300 or
more patrilineages
(*kulas*).

300 kulas

Each kula has 12-100
patrilineal segments.

12-100 lineages

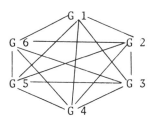

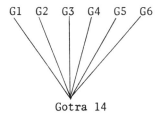

Inter-gata marriages
make possible 15 dif-
ferent alliance pat-
terns. G1-G2, G1-G3,
. . . , G5-G6.

Gotra 14 can marry with any
other gata or gotra.

While sibs are exogamous in South India, in Northern India there is an added marriage prohibition, a three or four-gotra rule of exogamy. A man may not marry a woman from his own gotra, or one from his mother's, his father's mother's, and sometimes (making the fourth) his mother's mother's. This rule has the effect of prohibiting marriage between persons related as closely as second cousins. In South India, there are usually no such prohibitions, and since cross-cousin marriage, or marriage with the mother's brother is allowed and even preferred, a minimal local lineage can repeat marriages with another minimal lineage, generation after generation. This has been referred to as a perpetual alliance. In both regions, the sub-caste is a connubium composed of a set of intermarrying sibs— either with no prohibitions with respect to renewal of ties from one generation to another, or with a prohibition requiring a minimum interruption of two or three generations.

Sib or Clan. In some parts of India the sib or clan, the exogamous unit within the jati, may be anchored *territorially* and represent a socially *organized* body with headmen and common property. Such is the *birādari* in parts of the northern state of Uttar Pradesh (Cohn 1968: 24), a set of males who believe themselves to be descended from a common male ancestor. They occupy a set of villages within a limited geographical territory which they hold by right of conquest or grant, having a political organization for self-government and relations with other social units such as the district or state government. M. C. Pradhan's study of the Jats of Meerut District is the most detailed study of such a clan, whose territory was called among his subjects a *khap*. Richard Fox has discussed a similar clan territorial and political organization for the Rajputs of Eastern Uttar Pradesh. It is such units which form regional dominant castes. (Fox 1971)

The Sub-Caste. Beyond the gotra or sib, there is seldom any conceptualization of segmentary unilineal relations. However, the combination of intermarrying sibs within an endogamous sub-caste makes the sub-caste, in effect, a descent-group. A number of sub-castes, be-

Figure 1.3
Caste is a Hierarchy of Increasingly Inclusive Segments

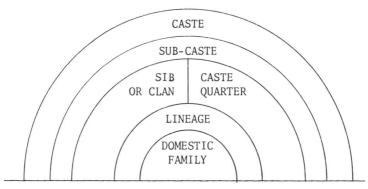

Segment	Function
Domestic Family	Commensality, procreation, early child care, work team, offerings to forebears and godlings, focus of life-cycle rites
Lineage	Neighboring with interfamilial support; elders arrange marriage for constituent families' youth; sharing of sacred food when a constituent family makes offerings to forebears and godlings; help and attendance at life-cycle rites of constiuent families; sharing of members' birth and death pollution.
Caste Quarter	Residence of constituent lineages; members form a "trade-union" supplying some service, craft or other benefit to other castes in locality; adult males form local caste council; worship of caste deities
Clan (or Sib)	Exogamy
Sub-caste	Endogamy; name; subculture; sometimes headmen
Caste	Common occupational specialty, name, and subculture (including myths, deities, history), closely-similar rank for constituent sub-castes.

tween which there is usually no conception of lineal
relations, form a caste. The sub-castes within a caste
usually share a common occupation, a common name, and
possibly some common cultural features. At the level
of the caste, the set of *cunnubia* (social units within
which marriages take place), or sub-castes, form an occupational group or an ethnic group. At this level of
the segmentary hierarchy, the unilineal principle
fails. Unification takes place because of similar
identity of occupation, name, and, sometimes, sub-
culture (myths, rituals, deities, religious teachers),
and ethnic history. The caste is not a socially
organized body. It is, rather, a social category.
Such categories were noted particularly by British
administrator-ethnographers (Cohn 1968: 24). The sub-
caste's unity is more in the eye of the beholder than
in the perception of the beheld. The administrator or
person of another caste usually sees all barbers in a
region, for example, as belonging to one caste, failing
to distinguish one sub-caste from another. If asked
his caste membership, the barber himself may give his
caste as his identity to a person of another caste; but
will probably give his sub-caste or gotra-title to a
member of his own caste.

The segmentation presented in Figure 1.3 is meant
to be more suggestive than exact, although it would
probably describe in an approximate pattern the structure of most castes. Others would have several additional segments based upon descent of a putative sort
or upon regional distribution. Also, not all anthropologists use the same terminology. Both Irawati Karve
and David Mandelbaum refer to the endogamous unit, the
jati, as the caste. In their terminology, the several
jatis composing a regional unity, with the same name,
occupation, and, possibly, ethnic history, are referred
to as a caste-cluster (Karve's term) or jati-cluster
(Mandelbaum's term) (Karve 1968: 9; Mandelbaum 1970:
17). Dumont and Ghurye use the term sub-caste for this
grouping, and sub-caste is the term used throughout
this book. (Dumont 1970; Ghurye 1961)

Until recent times, due to the difficulties of
travel in most parts of India, along with political,
linguistic, and geographical barriers—a jati was likely to have rather limited geographical spread. Thus,

for example, although there are Brahmans (traditionally household and temple priests, some of whom were learned in Sanskrit religious works) all over India, the Brahmans do not form a single jati. Even within the same region, there may be a number of different Brahman jatis. Enthoven reported in the Census of 1901 that the million and a half Brahmans of Bombay Province were divided into more than 200 groups between which marriage was forbidden (Census of India 1901, Volume ix, 278). In Tamilnadu, the Tamil Brahmans are divided into various groups usually referred to as sub-castes: the *Vadamās*, the *Vatimans*, the *Astāsahasrās*, and so on. Furthermore, these are divided into regional groups. There are *Choladesha Vadamās* and *Vadadesha Vadamās*, for example. The Cholodesha Vadamās are a jati originally located in the country of the ancient *Chola* kingdom, the valley of the Kaveri River. A Vadama will not marry a Vatiman, an Astasahasra, or a Vadadesha Vadama —only a Choladesha Vadama. From the point of view of a non-Brahman of Tamilnadu, all these are just Tamil Brahmans. It is of no importance to the non-Brahman that the Tamil Brahmans are sub-divided into various regional clusters and jatis.

There are a number of sizeable castes in India. Up-to-date census counts are not available; not since 1931 has the Census of India collected comprehensive data on caste membership. Max Weber pointed out that there were about twenty-five castes, diffused throughout most regions of India, which in 1911 composed over 40% of the population (at that time totaling 217 million). These included the Brahmans (14.6 million); Baniya (shopkeepers and merchants—1.12 million); Kayasths (traditionally official scribes—2.17 million); two castes of tribal origin—the Ahirs (now herdsmen—9.5 million), and Jats (now cultivating peasants—6.98 million); Untouchable Chamars (leather workers—11.5 million); Telis (oilpressers—4.27 million); Sonars (goldsmiths—1.26 million); Kumhars (potters—3.42 million); and Lohars (blacksmiths—2.07 million). (Weber 1958: 32)

A very large caste in Northwestern and West Central India is that of the Jats. These are excellent land cultivators, often held by British officials to be the best farmers in India. In fact, the Jat caste

is composed of a myriad jatis. Yet, as an example of
marriage restrictions, caste members from the tiny jati
of *Annana Jats*, located in Jaipur District of Rajasthan,
do not intermarry with the Sinsinwar Jats of Bharatpur
District just to the northeast, or to the Dholia Jats
of Ajmer District just to the southwest. Yet all are
Hindu Jats. Then, of course, there are Muslim Jats and
Sikh Jats; and within each religious category, there
are marriage restrictions among members of various
jatis.

The two features which link a series of sub-castes
into a caste are usually similarity in name and occupational function. There are, however, some castes which
include sub-castes varying in both function and caste
rank. A large caste in Karnataka state is the *Lingā-
yats*, originally formed from people of other castes who
converted to a religious sect, the *Virasaiva*. Among
the Lingayats are sub-castes of priests, merchants,
artisans, servants, and Untouchables. Thus, within the
caste of Lingayats, there is an entire complement of
specialists necessary for an operating caste system
(Dumont 1970: 189; Weber 1958: 19). Possibly converts
to the sect retained the specialty of their caste of
origin.

Another caste with sub-castes of varying function
and rank is the Nayars of Kerala, who were particularly
well-known as soldiers in the armies of various kings
of the area in pre-British times. They trace descent
matrilineally. High-ranking Nayar women mated with
Nambudiri Brahmans. The organization of the Nayar appears to be a kind of compromise between a caste and a
tribe. Among Nayars there are chiefly and commoner
sub-castes, the latter including a number of different
artisan and servant specialists (Gough 1959).

Thus the exact segmentary organization of castes
varies considerably. However, all castes are organized in terms of segments in a hierarchy of increasing
inclusiveness.

Chapter 2

The Origins of Caste

Following Durkheim's theory, Indian society was probably integrated at the tribal stage by "mechanical solidarity" (Durkheim 1893). In other words, the tribe was constructed over a framework of clans, the segments of which were culturally alike. Although some tribes might have a chief, shaman, or priest, there was minimal division of labor except by sex or age. The right to use force was held in a tribe "by the people in severalty" (Sahlins 1968: 5); every able-bodied adult male was a warrior, if need be. Considerations of kinship and obligation according to "lineage distance" (Evans-Pritchard 1940: 113) or corporate territory were supreme. Tribes were "kinship entities under lineage chiefs"—unlike states which were "territorial entities under public authorities." (Sahlins 1968)

It is not known exactly how rigid systems of stratification developed. Anthropologists, who seek to trace the evolution or "developmental trajectory" of social organizational types which have successively organized larger populations and more communities, see as crucial the emergence of a chief. Such an individual, often at first a ritual leader or war leader, is the focus for the accumulation of wealth. In the beginning he may merely redistribute the wealth to the populace during feasts or at tribal ceremonies.

The chiefdom is in the process of becoming a state when a chief can use some of the wealth contributed to his "bank" for other purposes. For example, he might spend a part of the wealth for the expense of a fleet of boats for trading and peace-making expeditions; or for an army; or for building public works; or for support of a priesthood, ministry, or bureaucracy.

The state, extending over a conquered territory, is ruled by a king whose subjects differ in rank. At this point two strata have often emerged—an aristocracy and commoners (Harris 1971: 392-401). In the process of state-formation, various craft and art specializations also develop, as well as some kind of land tax or tribute system to provide revenue for the monarch, his military, and his bureaucracy (Krader 1968).

The caste system of India, as a system of division of labor and land control, may have developed in the early kingdoms of northern India. Harold Gould in the module, *Caste and Class: A Comparative View*, shows the parallel in the development of the Indian division of labor, embodied in the caste system, with developments of division of labor in other ancient states. What makes the Indian caste system unique is the feature of closed endogamous descent-groups as the social unit for occupational specialization. This feature has no parallel in other societies. Louis Dumont has tried to explain the development of closed endogamous descent-groups on the basis of the principle of purity and pollution. (See Chapter 4.)

THE INDUS VALLEY CIVILIZATION

Ancient City Dwellers—The Harappan Civilization.
Archeological evidence reveals the existence of cities in northwestern South Asia (now largely West Pakistan) at a very early date. There were well-developed cities located in the valley of the Indus River in 2500 B.C. This suggests that by that time a state or chiefdoms had already developed. This Indus or *Harappan Civilization* was one of the most ancient civilizations in the world—coexisting with those of Sumer, Northern China, and Egypt, but much more extensive in area than any of these.

The Harappan civilization lasted at least 400 years (Allchin and Allchin 1968: 140). Over two hundred sites, including villages, towns, and four cities, have been excavated (Begley 1975). The distribution of the sites (located mostly in presentday West Pakistan, but also extending southward into Gujarat and eastward into Rajasthan, the Punjab, and Uttar Pradesh in India) covers at least 500,000 square miles (Allchin and Allchin 1968: 127-128). The map on page 26 shows the extent of the Indus Valley Civilization.

Excavations reveal carefully-planned cities and towns with streets laid out in grid-fashion over well-constructed drainage. The city plan was adhered to over long periods of time, new construction coinciding with the old. There were public buildings, including in each community a "citadel" on a high platform, and a public granary. The uniformity of architecture, settlement plan, and artifacts (including standard weights and measures) in sites hundreds of miles apart has baffled archeologists. The archeologist V. Gordon Childe expressed this puzzlement when he wrote about the cities of Mohenjo-daro, Chanhu-daro on the Indus River, and Harappa, on the Ravi River four hundred miles away.

> Yet the civilization of all three is astonishingly homogeneous; all the specific idiosyncrasies of architecture and town planning, of metal tools and weapons, of ornaments and beads, of art and epigraphy noted at Mohenjo-daro recur at Harappa . . . And the agreement is not a simple uniformity explicable by parallel developments under similar environmental conditions, but something much more artificial, expressed, for instance, in the identity of a highly individualized and self-conscious ceramic and glyptic art . . . Identically the same civilization has been found downstream to Amri and upstream it is reported as far as Rupar on the Upper Sutlej. The area embraced by the Indus civilization in the Harappa period must have been twice that of Old Kingdom Egypt and probably four times that of Sumer and Akkad.
>
> (Childe 1953: 173)

Archeologists disagree about the cultural affinities of the Indus people. Physical remains are mixed, including Australoid, Mediterranean, Alpine, and Mongoloid types of human skeletons, so that the remains are not diagnostic (Childe 1953: 175). A script which

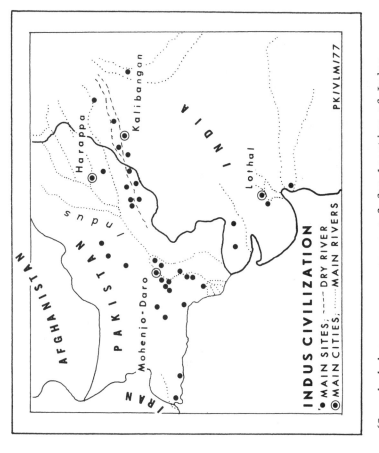

INDUS CIVILIZATION
• MAIN SITES; --- DRY RIVER
⊙ MAIN CITIES; ⋯⋯ MAIN RIVERS

PK/VLM/77

(See shaded area on map on page 2 for location of Indus Valley on South Asian Peninsula.)

occurs very largely on square steatite seals has not yet been definitively deciphered. A dozen or more European and South Asian scholars have worked on the decipherment in recent years. Most favor the hypothesis that it was a written form of proto(early)-Dravidian. Thus these city-dwellers may have been ancestors of the speakers of the Dravidian family of languages. These people now populate South India and form pockets of tribesmen in Central and South India, as well.

A Theocracy Rather than an Empire. There is no archeological proof of the existence in the Harappan Civilization of a king or a standing army (Fairservis 1971: 299-300; Piggott 1950: 273), or of the existence of a kingdom or empire (Allchin and Allchin 1968: 129). Indeed, very few weapons have been discovered in the excavations (Childe 1953: 181). Although irrigation was important for the agriculture of the area, it may not have been organized by a central state but may have been organized in small systems on local bases. The presence of huge granaries, such as the one at Harappa which was 168 feet by 135 feet (Childe 1953: 174), suggests that wealth was accumulated by some civil authorities (Fairservis 1971: 250, 252, 265-266), who might then have redistributed it. There is evidence of wide-ranging trade and river transportation.

Elman Service, the cultural evolutionary anthropologist, has suggested that the Indus Civilization was a theocracy rather than a conquest state or empire. The various elements of the planned Indus cities were probably developed before the cities were established. Thus the cities may have been built as civic-ceremonial centers. The absence of weaponry, the lack of defensive walls, and the scattered location of villages suggest that there was little or no warfare. Thus, like Egypt, the Indus civilization may have been a theocracy, a state unified by a priesthood rather than by a kingly conqueror (Service 1975: 238-246).

The Indian archeologist S. C. Malik has argued that the Indus was not a state, but a set of chiefdoms. Such chiefdoms may have become regionally specialized in production of commodities, each chief serving as the center of a redistributive network (Service 1975: 243). Malik sees castes as possibly having developed out of chiefdoms. It is not unusual for an aristocracy—the chiefly stratum—to close rank and become endogamous. Such segmental endogamy might have spread to occupational specialists of lower rank within the chiefdom. (Malik 1968: 99-110)

Evidence of Early Social Classes. Castes also might have developed out of social classes. This is suggested by the differences in house-type in the Indus cities. Some houses were small two-room affairs, while others were large two-story mansions (Allchin and Allchin 1968: 242; Fairservis 1971: 256, 292, 299, 300). Occupational specialization is suggested by the evidence of trade, including commerce by seagoing vessels (Allchin and Allchin 1968: 272; Fairservis 1971: 278, 280). Artifacts point to the presence of craftsmen making beads, seals, bricks, pottery, and faience, and working on copper, silver, gold, bronze, stone, shell, and bone (Allchin and Allchin 1968: 268; Fairservis 1971: 261, 299).

Clearly, there were occupational specialists in Harappan society, but nothing is known of the social organization of such specialists. Were they closed, endogamous descent-groups like the later jatis?

Piggott, an archeologist, has suggested that the conservatism of Harappan culture, its uniformity over centuries and over hundreds of miles, must have been maintained through religious sanctions (Piggott 1950: 150-151). Fairservis suggests that this was an earlier version of the later Hindu concept of *dharma* (religious defined duty, so that every role in society had its dharma). The concept of dharma, however, is Aryan in origin and prevailed 2000 years after the Indus civilization. It is likely that the Harappan specialists held some ideology which justified the worthiness of their "trade" and that Harappan culture was integrated by some stabilizing shared values.

Were There Purity-Pollution Concepts in the Indus Civilization? Shower baths were regular features of Indus homes, and one of the major finds at Mohenjo-daro is a large bathing ghat, similar in structure to those used by Hindus. The showers, the bathing ghat, and the elaborate system of underground drainage are not found

elsewhere in the ancient world, and suggest that the
Indus people were preoccupied with cleanliness and
bathing. It has also been suggested that this was an
early form of the Hindu Purity-Pollution complex which
is described in detail in Chapter 4.

Hindu Gods at Indus Sites? Various of the images un-
earthed in the archeological excavations appear to be
similar to those of later Hinduism. Huge stone *phalli*
with rings look like the *lingam* and *yoni* by which the
great Hindu god, Shiva, is often worshipped. A seal
found at Mohenjo-daro showing a horned figure with
three faces sitting in the "lotus-position" of the
Hindu holy man may be an early form of the Hindu god
Shiva, and has been dubbed a "proto-Shiva." Female
figures of clay may be the early mother-goddesses,
widely worshipped later by Hindus (Childe 1953: 184-
185). Since neither Shiva nor the mother-goddesses
appear in the Aryan religious works, cultural historians believe such Hindu gods may have originated in
the Indus Valley culture. Whether social institutions,
such as caste, or basic cultural concepts, such as
dharma, were similarly transmitted is very difficult to
prove.

VEDIC SOCIETY AND CULTURE

Hinduism and the Hindu caste system emerged from a
blending of the culture of the Aryans and the cultures
of the people already resident in northern India, probably including the descendants of the sophisticated
city-dwellers of the Indus Valley. The Aryans were
nomadic pastoral warriors, organized in tribes, who
entered northwestern India around 1500 B.C., their
forebears having come from Northern Eurasia (Wasson
1968: 209). The Aryan tribes, governed by a chief
(*rājā*) and two councils, were already composed of two
social classes—the nobility and commoners. The chief
was primarily a war leader (Basham 1954: 33). He was
aided by a general and a priest, the predecessor of
the later Brahman priesthood. The Aryan tribes were
subdivided into patrilineages with depths of from four
to thirteen generations. For example, the *gotra* of the

holy text of the Aryans, the *Rig Veda*, was an "exogamous non-localized patrilineal sib"—that is, a set of
male relatives who believed themselves to be descended
from a common male ancestor although actual linkages
could not be remembered and traced (patrilineal sib).
Gotra members resided in various localities, so they
were dispersed and non-localized. They were exogamous
—required to marry women of other sibs. The residential unit was a group of patrilineally related men—the
grāma. The kinship terminology characteristic of these
early Aryans (labeled as Omaha by anthropologists) was
"typical of the patrilineate in its most highly developed form" (White 1939: 240, quoted by Friedrich 1966:
29).

The Aryans (1500-500 B.C.). Aryans were uncivilized in
that they did not live in cities and did not have writing. As warriors, however, they used superior weaponry
and swift horse-drawn chariots. Over the centuries
they moved gradually across the North Indian plain—
conquering the indigenous peoples, clearing the ground
as they went with their slash-and-burn agriculture.
The chief or raja became more powerful, as did the
Brahmans who performed for him complicated sacrificial
rites with a sophisticated poetry preserved in a highly
self-conscious oral tradition. This religious poetry
was called the Vedas. It is from the Vedas that our
knowledge of the Aryans largely comes. The hymns are
addressed to a group of nature deities on behalf of the
warriors and their priests. By the late Vedic period
(1000-500 B.C.), the Aryans had established little
kingdoms across the Gangetic Plain, and tribal organization based on kinship had given way to territorial
political units.

CULTURES COMBINED: HINDUISM

The working together of the Aryan culture and cultures
of the indigenous conquered peoples produced Hinduism
and the caste system with the Brahman at its apex as
priest. Both Hinduism and the caste system had been
established by the pre-Christian era and had spread
from northern India to the southern part of the penin-

sula (Sastri 1963: 28)—absorbing and eventually winning out over such sophisticated competitors as Buddhism and Jainism. Thus the historical process was one of progressive Hinduization of tribes. Those tribes closer to centers of Aryan rule were integrated into the Hindu social order first; those further distant being integrated later (Stein 1969). Some resistors, unwilling to conform to Hinduism and caste, withdrew to economically-marginal areas. The most remote tribes, such as those in the northeastern mountains, withstood Hinduization more successfully than those in the peninsula.

As early as the eighth century B.C., Hindu thought had separated worldly power from other-worldly power. Since then, the two realms have been in the hands of different specialists—worldly power in the hands of the king, other-worldly power in the hands of the priest. In the Hindu ideology, the ritual power of the Brahman priest was more important than the secular power of the king, who was expected to protect and depend upon the priest (Dumont 1970: 70-71). Indeed, it was the duty of the king (raja) to protect the populace, to ensure conformity to the class system of the time, and to wage war—always under the guidance of his Brahman (priestly) preceptor. The king was carrying out the religious law (dharma) that was in the keeping of the Brahman priest.

Any aristocracy must have an ideology justifying its superior standing, as well as the lesser standings of other lower classes in a system of stratification. Such an ideology must rest upon ideas held generally by the members of the society. In other words, the high rank of the elite must be acceptable to the non-elite in terms of values to which they themselves are committed. An extensive religious literature of great antiquity supports the pre-eminence of the Brahman. The charter for the social classes in ancient India is found in the tenth *mandala* (circle) of the holy text, the *Rig Veda*. This charter awards highest rank to the Brahman priest. The passage concerns the sacrifice of a superman whose mouth became the *brāhman* priest, whose two arms formed the *rājanya* warrior, whose two thighs formed the *vaishya* landowners and merchants, and from whose feet were born the *shudra* artisans and servants (deBary *et al.* 1958: 17).

These four classes, called *varnas*, seem to have existed in the Aryan society in ancient northern India. The members of the three higher varnas were probably mostly Aryans, while the Shudras were probably mostly darker-skinned, conquered peoples. Later, there developed a so-called "fifth" varna who were Untouchables.

It is generally agreed by scholars of ancient India that the varnas of Aryan society were functional groupings rather than closed endogamous birth-descent groups. That is, the original varnas were *not* jatis or castes, for there is evidence that people could and did change their varna identity. Furthermore, marriages between persons of different varnas took place and were allowed (Basham 1954: 146-147; Ghurye 1961: 52-53).

The fixity of caste membership came about later, possibly with the development and acceptance of the Hindu pollution complex of beliefs; or possibly with the Hindu belief of rebirth. Neither of these concepts were Aryan ideas, and perhaps came into the new amalgamated religion of Hinduism (dating from 250 B.C.) from the conquered people. If one believed in reincarnation, one saw one's place in the caste system as reflective of one's character in a previous life. If one was reborn an Untouchable, one had, obviously, been more sinful than if one was reborn a Brahman.

The highest three varnas—the priests, the warriors, and herder-cultivators (later merchants)—were called the "twice-born," referring to the Sacred Thread Ceremony at the start of a boy's religious studies. Like many adolescent initiation rites throughout the world, the ceremony was imaged as a second birth. Presumably, a boy was equivalent in status to a shudra (a member of the servant varna, the lowest varna) until his Sacred Thread Ceremony. Shudra and Untouchable boys were not allowed to study or even to hear the sacred texts. In fact, until thirty years ago one of the justifications for prohibiting lower castes from the Brahman streets in South India was this prohibition —they might overhear Brahmans chanting Sanskrit religious verses.

THE VARNA, JATI, CASTE RELATIONSHIP

What is the relationship between the varnas and jatis and castes? There is some historical evidence of transitional social segments, part-jati, part-varna. The existence in northern India of classes which have the shape of the varnas, but also some of the characteristics of jatis is indicated in the observation of Megasthenes, the ambassador from the Greek colony of Bactria (located in present-day Afghanistan), sent to the court of Chandra Gupta Maurya (322-298 B.C.) in his capital, *Pataliputra* (presentday Patna, Bihar). Megasthenes reported that the population of the earliest great Hindu empire, the Mauryan, was divided into seven endogamous, craft-exclusive classes:

1. Philosophers, who offered sacrifices and performed rituals

2. Husbandmen, who made up the largest proportion of the population

3. Shepherds and hunters

4. Workers at trades, vendors, laborers

5. Fighting men

6. Inspectors

7. Councillors and assessors of the king

(McCrindle 1877: 83-86)

While Megasthenes never mentioned the varnas of the ancient religious texts, the seven classes do correspond to the four varnas (philosophers are the Brahmans, husbandmen are the Vaishya, workers at trades are Shudras, and fighting men are Kshatriyas), plus the tribals (shepherds and hunters), and plus two categories of royal bureaucrats (the secret police being equivalent to the inspectors, and the king's cabinet, administrators, and tax agents being the councillors and assessors).

Such an interpretation may or may not be completely correct. However, the characteristics of *endogamy* and *craft-exclusiveness*, involving a prohibition

on changing occupation (except for a special dispensa-
tion for the "philosophers"), are features characteristic of caste systems. The fact that these two features
were noteworthy in Indian society at so early a time as
the third century B.C. is significant.
There is considerable early evidence of occupational specialization, and of Untouchables. Buddhist
Pāli scriptures from centuries before Christ refer to
separate villages of Brahmans, potters, hunters, and
robbers. In cities, there were separate sections for
different occupational groups, many of which were organized into guilds (Basham 1954: 149). There is relatively little mention of jatis in ancient Hindu and
Buddhist religious writing, although some named groups
appear to be jatis; these are mostly low-ranking or
untouchable groups, said to be descendants of the offspring of intervarna marriages. In ancient texts, dis-
cussion of the social categories used in the society of
the time is in terms of varnas (Basham 1954: 148; Dumont
1970: 68, 71). In what century did the jatis finally
prevail as endogamous, craft-exclusive, socially separated, but economically- and ritually-interdependent
groups? Scholars disagree. Dumont believes that Indian society was already organized in jatis by the
third century A.D., when the writers of the law books
were discoursing on varnas (Dumont 1970: 68). Basham,
on the other hand, believes there to be no evidence for
such social units as the jatis until the ninth century
A.D. (Basham 1954: 148). He points out that during the
Gupta dynasty, when one kingdom spread over much of
northern India, there were intervarna marriages; craft
exclusiveness was often ignored; and Brahmans accepted
food from anyone considered to be Aryan (presumably in
the top three varnas). These are all indications, according to Basham, that the rigid closures of the caste
system had not yet been established.
      Ancient Hindu law books suggest that jatis,
(closed endogamous descent-groups, usually with an occupational specialization) developed out of intervarna
marriages. Ancient kings were directed by the law
books to prevent intervarna marriage, but evidently it
did occur. The relative standing of the offspring of
such marriages depended upon the combination of varnas
of the parents. Thus, the child of a man of higher

varna and a woman of lower varna (a hypergamous marriage) had a status midway between that of both parents. The exception was the child of a Brahman father and a Shudra mother, who was held to be impure. The child of a Brahman mother and a lower varna father, on the other hand, was a *Candāla*, or Untouchable.

Historians of ancient India generally reject this theory of intervarna marriage as the explanation for the development of the jatis. Possibly the varna ideal contributed to the idea of occupational specialization, but jatis seem to have developed as in-migrating groups, tribal groups, or groups with a newly developed craft were integrated into a single social system. Each, as a closed segment, was ranked in a local complement of jatis or castes. As Dumont has said, Hindus "will assign a rank, where we in the West would approve or exclude" (Dumont 1970: 191). Irawati Karve has also emphasized the caste system as a social device for integrating varying in-migrating tribal or ethnic groups (Karve 1968).

Concern with the impurities of human organic life and the impurities of caste seem to have developed together. The *Laws of Manu*, which date at latest third century A.D., refer to impurity from outcasted persons, as well as from birth, death, and menstruation (Dumont 1970: 53). The Chinese Buddhist pilgrim, Fa-hsien, reported that during his visit to Buddha's homeland in northern India, in the fourth century A.D., most people were vegetarians, and that meat-eating was reserved to low castes and to Untouchables. He refers to "pollution on approach"—that is, pollution from coming close to an Untouchable or outcast (Basham 1954: 66). During these early times, leather workers (today many Untouchables are leather workers) were already disliked, as evidenced by their being heavily taxed (Basham 1954: 107). The Candalas, an early Untouchable group, had to prepare the dead for cremation. They were considered inauspicious for others and lived on other people's refuse. In one of the Buddhist *Jātaka* tales, a Brahman eats food from a Candala and goes off into the forest to die (Basham 1954: 176; Dumont 1970: 52-53), because such internal pollution could not be expunged.

In Jan Breman's study of the caste system of two villages in southern Gujarat, it becomes evident how a tribal group gradually becomes a caste—in this case, that of the *Dublas*, an Untouchable caste. These tribal people became agricultural laborers for the land-controlling Anavil Brahmans. Besides doing work in the fields, they also did other kinds of "filthy" work that only Untouchables would do. Their willingness to do so is presumably accounted for by the absence in their tribal culture of the pollution complex of Hinduism. Once settled in Hindu villages, however, they are treated as Untouchables because of the pollution attitudes of their Hindu patrons and neighbors (Breman 1974: 256).

J. A. Baines suggested that as Brahmans settled in a region, a system of land servitude developed, in which the indigenous tribal people became the servants of the Brahman, who was not allowed by religious proscription to put his hand to the plow (J. A. Baines 1912, quoted by Breman 1974: 39).

Thus the caste system seems to have come about as a multiplicity of ethnic groups accepted hierarchical ordering, social isolation, and in-breeding sanctioned by the belief that ritual pollution would result from inter-caste sexual relations. Integration into a ranked series of strata was the price which a group had to pay in order to settle in an agricultural village. The historical sociologist Barrington Moore said:

> Thus caste was and indeed remains tremendously persistent and tremendously flexible, in its concrete manifestation, a huge mass of locally co-ordinated social cells that tolerate novelty by generating another cell.
>
> (Moore 1966: 340)

Marriott and Inden concur about the caste process of ordering a multiplicity of groups by ranking. They also suggest as above, that this process is more usual in small-scale societies than in large-scale ones.

> Caste systems are comparatively rare among large-scale moral systems in making the differentiation and interrelations of corporate groups into major concerns; but in this they are at one with a large and diverse category of small-scale societies.
>
> (Marriott and Inden 1973: 982)

Chapter 3

The Caste System Analyzed: The Localized Social Structure

EARLY WESTERN VIEW OF THE CASTE SYSTEM

One of the earliest European observers to write about the Hindu caste system in the modern period was the sixteenth century Portuguese, Duarte Barbosa. He saw quite clearly the key features of the system—the high position of Brahmans, the importance of pollution and untouchability, the separation of endogamous groups from each other through prohibitions upon commensality (eating together), the occupational feature of castes, the self-governing of castes, and the relationship between castes and politics (Cohn 1968: 5).

During the eighteenth and nineteenth centuries, some Europeans became oriental scholars and translated Hindu and Buddhist texts. They brought to the attention of the Western intellectual community the rich religious and philosophical heritage of South Asia. Max Muller, one of the leading orientalists, registered the surprise that greeted the realization that the caste system as it existed at the time was not justified by the ancient Hindu texts. There was a scheme of ancient social classes called varnas to be found in the texts, but *not* a description or ideology for the caste system (Max Muller 1858: 299-317). However, the eighteenth and nineteenth century British missionaries and orientalists, influenced by the ancient texts, tended to emphasize the superiority of the Brahmans through their

effective monopoly over religious knowledge. However,
the Westerners were mistaken in suggesting that the
Brahmans' religious suzerainty was also a political
dominance. Finally, in 1908 the French sociologist,
Célestin Bouglé, distinguished the two kinds of power
in his book on the caste system (Bouglé 1908).

The early missionaries and orientalists also accepted the varna theory and the explanation that castes
had developed from intervarna marriages. Indeed, they
seemed to believe the "proof" of the ancient texts,
rather than the observations based on their own experiences in India. The lack of fit between the class system described in ancient texts and the caste system
they observed, if they noted the discrepancy at all,
was attributed to the degeneration of an ancient order
(Cohn 1968: 10).

Later nineteenth century and early twentieth century writers on the caste system were especially im-
pressed with the occupational specialization of castes.
John C. Nesfield explained the origins of the caste
system as a process of evolution of occupations (Nesfield 1885). Again, the French sociologist Bouglé
has criticized such a theory—pointing out that although caste occupations are important, the hierarchy
of castes is not so much a hierarchy of skills as a
hierarchy of pollution (Bouglé 1971: 29-40). Purity-
impurity, as the decisive principle of the caste hierarchy, continues to be asserted by Bouglé's disciple,
Louis Dumont (1970), as we have noted in the previous
chapter.

The ancient religious texts reiterated the Hindu
principles of reincarnation and *karma*, the idea that
one is reborn over and over again in stations determined by one's past action. If, in a past life, one
had been meritorious, then one might be reborn a high-
ranking Brahman priest. If one had been sinful, then
one might be reborn a lowly Untouchable. Max Weber,
the influential German sociologist, identified this belief as the justifying ideology of the caste system
(Weber 1958: 118). Such scholars seemed to assume that
religious texts both regulated and explained an existing social structure of castes. They seldom asked
whether living Hindus knew and believed these ancient
teachings. Unfortunately, the anthropologists seldom
had (or have now) the data to answer this question.

It is of note that the low-ranking varna of Shudras was specifically excluded by the Hindu law books from studying or hearing the sacred texts. In reality, very few of the equivalent low castes have had access to such teaching. This leaves open to question whether the theory of rebirth and karma functioned to make the lower castes resigned to their fate. In fact, the theory probably functioned mainly to make the high castemen, who identified themselves as members of a high varna, pleased with their status.

During the nineteenth century and early twentieth century, British ethnographers tended to merge castes with tribes. The titles of the volumes they edited were often "Tribes and Castes of X Region." Many of these ethnographers were employed by the Census of India. Unlike the textually-inspired Sanskrit schol-ars, they drew on empirical observation, either their own or that of others. They observed castes as unrelated ethnic groups—each with its own occupational, religious, and social customs. Weighty compendia compiled by these diligent men are now referred to by scholars seeking knowledge about the peoples of India as they were under British rule (1757-1947). These Census ethnographers failed to see that a caste *system* is a set of interrelated parts (castes). They are faulted by today's scholars for their tendency to homogenize information, to combine samples of fact about a people all bearing the same tribal or caste label—seemingly unconcerned about details of place or time, or about problems of representativeness of any fact cited in terms of the whole population of the tribe or caste in question. (See Blunt 1931; Crooke 1896; Enthoven 1920-22; Hutton 1963; Ibbetson 1916; Thurston 1909).

CONTEMPORARY SOCIAL ANTHROPOLOGISTS VIEW
THE CASTE SYSTEM

Since the late 1940s, a number of Indian, British, and American social scientists have taken a new approach to the Indian caste system. The dominant features of this approach are inspired by modern social anthropology. The first important feature is the collection of information about the caste system by residing in, observing, and participating in the ongoing life of an Indian community, usually a village, sometimes a rural caste community, or less often, a small region. Second, these social scientists focus upon life as it is being lived at present, supplemented by whatever historical information might have been recorded in gazetteers or elsewhere referring to the local region. Third, a holistic approach is taken. In other words, caste relations are treated as just one aspect of Indian life. Other influential aspects might be the family life, religion, kinship, economics, and politics within a social structure studied within a locality. Fourth, examination of social relations *between* castes and *within* local caste segments is made. Fifth, the anthropologist often draws the boundaries of a caste *system* as coinciding with the boundaries of a village, even though this may give the impression that the village is more of an isolate than it is when inter-village contacts and supravillage social networks are taken into consideration. Notable examples of such village studies include Dube 1955; Berreman 1963; Srinivas 1955; Gough 1955, 1960; Dumont 1954; Lewis 1958; Mayer 1960. For *caveats* see Opler 1956; Lewis 1955; Dumont 1966.

From such studies there has emerged an image of the Indian caste system which includes the following components:

1. Caste as a *system* operates only within a limited locality, a single village or a few linked villages.

2. A village or local population is composed of a series of mutually exclusive castes, usually numbering anywhere from a handful to a score or more.

3. A dominant caste, or a dominant family, or set of families, typically has preponderant political and economic power over everyone else in the locality. Dominance is rooted in monopolistic control over arable land and in physical force.

4. Each caste has an occupational specialty, and offers this to other castes in exchange for food, products, or services. Especially important is the food grain provided by the land-controlling dominant caste or families to the landless serv-

ant, artisan, and mendicant castes. This exchange of food, goods, and services is a ritual system concerned with purity and pollution as well as an economic system. Called the *jajmāni* system, it functions so that the highest castes remain pure while the lower castes absorb pollution for them.

5. Castes within a local caste system tend to be mutually ranked according to their respective degrees of pollution in this ritual system.

6. Efforts to improve caste rank in this local caste hierarchy are made by middle and lower castes, especially by means of discarding polluting customs, and by emulating the customs of the higher purer castes.

7. Political power is monopolized by the dominant caste, family, or families, or occasionally by a pair of competing dominant castes. Non-dominant castes tend to support their patrons within the dominant segment. Such support may be important if there are factions contending for power within the dominant segment.

8. Disputes may be settled either by councils within a caste segment, or by one or more elders of the dominant caste or family.

9. The caste segment itself is an endogamous descent-group. The local contingent of a caste is usually composed of kinsmen, ideally related unilineally, though often actually related cognatically. (Patrilineal descent refers to a line of males related through father-son links, going back to a common male ancestor. Matrilineal descent refers to a line of mother-child links, going back to a common female ancestor. Cognatic descent refers to a line, related through either male or female links, going back to common ancestors.)

10. Each caste segment tends to live in its own quarter. Universally, Untouchables (who are unclean) live in isolation from those of purer caste, either in a separate hamlet or on the outskirts of a village.

To describe caste as a system, these features will be elaborated.

THE DOMINANT CASTE

Rarely in Indian history was most of the Indian subcontinent united under a single ruler. Perhaps only a half dozen times from the Mauryan Empire (322-183 B.C.) until the British unification in the nineteenth century (by 1857) of about two-thirds of the peninsula, did such singular rule occur. Thus, India was united under one ruler for only a few hundred years during three millenia.

The more usual situation was rule by a plethora of petty rulers contending with each other in the various regions of the subcontinent. A number of scholars have emphasized the irrelevance to the village or local society of a supreme government (Basham 1954: 151; Dumont 1970: 156; Moore 1966: 315). The supreme ruler needed grain from the villages to support his army, and so the government was an agency demanding its share of the harvest. Even under the Moghul Empire (1526-1757) and under the British, the central government intruded into village life almost entirely for the purpose of revenue collection. Both empires left local rule in the hands of dominant castes or dominant clans, and to the local caste councils.

A dominant caste may dominate a set of contiguous or closely related villages. Sometimes a *single clan* of a dominant caste controls a number of villages in an area, so that a petty state or clandom exists. A branch of the clan resides in each village, and the superiority of a clan-head over all in the village is recognized. M. G. Pradhan has described a Jat clan territory of this type in Western Uttar Pradesh. Richard Fox has described one for a Rajput clan of Eastern Uttar Pradesh (M. C. Pradhan 1966; Fox 1971).

However, a dominant caste is not organized on any higher level than that of a clandom, or in the past, a petty state. Thus, there did not develop in India a national aristocracy recognizing its common class interests. Dominance and rule were highly fragmented. This fragmentation of Indian society meant that there was no organization of the myriad dominant castes into one dominant caste or into a few intra-communicating communities or classes.

The prohibition on marriage across caste lines effectively insulated one dominant caste from another. Local leaders with peasant followings fought Moghul emperors locally and often effectively, but the fragmented efforts meant a gradual disintegration of the Moghul empire with no adequately-organized power to take its place. Contrast this situation with the situations in feudal Europe or feudal Japan where local ruling lords or gentry did organize together against a central ruler—with the ultimate effect of furthering both political and economic modernization. Only recently, through the auspices of central and state legislation and the pan-Indian Community Development Program have men of the dominant castes been taking on the role of rural agricultural modernizers. And only within the past century, as a result of improved transportation and communication, have castes begun to organize into larger-scale regional associations—caste associations.

To describe the caste system as it exists in India today, it is necessary to understand that the system, as it operates in most villages, is an inheritance from a period when a martial caste protected other castes, when there was continual warfare between rulers or clans as they struggled for territory, tribute, and supporters. In such a situation, a local social structure developed which centered about a dominant caste, or dominant family, or families.

M. N. Srinivas first introduced the concept of "dominant caste." In the Mysore village he described, the peasant Okkaligas composed nearly half of a population made up of nineteen jāti groups. The Okkaligas were the biggest landowners; they dominated all other castes economically and politically, as well as numerically. However, they had only middle rank ritually and were surpassed in purity by both Brahmans and Lingayats (Srinivas 1955).

Gough (1955), who studied a Tamil village dominated by Brahmans, Srinivas, and others have emphasized the importance of the dominant caste in settling disputes between persons of both their own and of other jatis. The power of the dominant caste is supported by a norm discouraging villagers from seeking justice from area government officials, courts, or police located outside the village. This reliance on the village is justified supposedly by an ideal of preserving the village's reputation for harmony and virtue. Members of the dominant caste, particularly those from wealthy and/or powerful families, are the representatives of the village in dealings with government officials and other prestigious outsiders. Elected self-governing local councils (*panchayats*) have been established all over India since Independence in 1947, and where a dominant caste has sufficient numbers, it has usually been able to occupy a number of positions on the elected village council.

Other Patterns of Village Organization. Besides rule by a dominant caste, there are other patterns of village organization. A village or set of villages may be controlled by a single individual or family; this was the usual pattern in the princely states until recent years. A maharaja granted *jagirs*, rights to receive a portion of the crops produced by tenant cultivators, to *jagirdars*. In return, the jagirdars were expected to support the maharaja personally and to supply him with such facilities as tribute and a certain number of equipped troops. Brij Raj Chauhan's *Rajasthan Village* (1967) is a study of a *jagirdari* village. Shamirpet, in the former princely state of Hyderabad, studied by S. C. Dube, is another (1955). Jagirdari rights have now been abolished and the land in such villages is owned by the dominant caste which was previously the tenants of the jagirdar. Even as tenants, such land-controlling castes had been dominant locally.

Since India became independent of British rule in 1947, there have been various land reform measures which have terminated the land rights, particularly of absentee landlords. In most villages, the dominant caste had lost little land, and in some cases it has increased its land holding by acquiring the rights of the absent landlords.

In villages or regions with dominant castes, it is usually only a portion of the families or lineages which hold the decisive politico-economic power (Mayer

1958). Where a dominant caste does not have a numerical preponderance over all other jati-groups or where the caste lacks decisive economic control, its political power depends upon support from other jatis. For example, in a village in Central India studied by Adrian Mayer, the dominant Rajput group was supported by four "allied castes" with whom the Rajputs were willing to dine and to treat as their equals. The Rajputs' right to dominance, however, derived from their occupancy of three hereditary headships. Until recently, the headmen were closely associated with the maharaja for whom they collected revenue and performed other duties. With post-Independence reforms, the maharaja has lost his rights, so the Rajputs now are a dominant caste with complete independence (Mayer 1960; 36-38, 92).

A dominant caste may or may not hold such hereditary offices of leadership or responsibility. Within a village or region, it is not uncommon for two castes to be "rivals for dominance" (Beck 1972; Orenstein 1965).

Factions Within the Dominant Caste. Dominant castes typically are divided internally into various rival factions which contend with each other for power, property, influence, and prestige. The form of factionalization within a village depends largely upon the number of members of a dominant jati and upon the pattern of land distribution. Land control in the hands of one man may lead to a situation of a single powerful headman to whom everyone else is subordinate. If land control is widely dispersed among members of a large dominant jati, then factions tend to be "vertical"—between segments of the dominant jati, joined by their respective dependents from other jatis (Nicholas 1968).

Intercaste factionalism is unusual and is probably recent. It tends to take place when a dominant jati is small, and there is another jati present which is sizeable, although lower-ranking. The ability of the latter to compete has emerged with the establishment of universal franchise and democratic elections in 1952, as well as certain laws protecting lower castes. Officials, police, and courts willing to enforce such laws are essential if the lower caste contenders are to succeed, however.

THE HINDU JAJMANI SYSTEM

A Sample Village: Khalapur.* Caste operates as a system only locally. To explain the caste system, the *jajmani* system and the *hali* system must be understood. The jajmani system will be examined through the example of the village of Khalapur in northwestern Uttar Pradesh, located in the rich sliver of land between the two rivers, the Ganges and the Jumna. In the mid-1950s, Khalapur had a population of over 5,000 persons divided into 31 jatis.

Khalapur is typical of the village integrated by a dominant caste. The anthropologist Srinivas said that the dominant caste in a village or region had decisive economic and political power, and usually had a fairly high ritual rank—that is, the dominant caste was one of the purer castes. Dominance was even stronger if the caste was the largest jati-group present, if it had some members in the active leadership who had had a Western education, and if the caste was a part of a jati-group or larger caste dominating an extensive geographical area. Rarely does a dominant caste have all of these dominance features (Srinivas 1955, 1959).

The Rajputs of Khalapur had most of them—a numerical preponderance, since they composed 42 percent of the village population in 1954; economic power, since they owned and controlled 90 percent of the village land; political power, since the lower castes all had to do their bidding. They did not have the highest ritual status. They ranked below the Brahmans, but the Brahmans had none of the other characteristics for dominance, being few in number and relatively poor. There were at least two men in one of the larger Rajput patrilineages who knew some English (Hitchcock 1960). Khalapur is not located in a tract dominated by Rajputs, but it is one of ten villages in the area held by Rajput descendants of the same male ancestor (Hitchcock 1971: 175).

In Khalapur, the other jatis said that the village "belonged to the Rajputs." The cultural formula for explaining the presence of the other jati-groups was that the Rajputs had invited one family or more of each of the other jatis to settle in Khalapur, so that services and products would be provided for them.

---

*See map on page 2 for location of Khalapur.

Those with "might" have certain "rights," or at least high status. A politically dominant caste is likely to have high ritual rank even though it has a traditional occupation of warrior, and its men eat meat and consume alcoholic liquors. So, in Khalapur, in the overall ranking of castes, the Rajputs were ranked second, below only the Brahmans. In Khalapur, villagers were asked what gestures expressing pollution they would allow persons of other castes to make with respect to themselves. If a caste member was allowed to make the gesture, then the caste was of a higher rank in the eyes of the villager. Thus, respondents were asked from which castes they would take water, boiled food, fried food, who could smoke their *hukka*-pipes, whose touch they would object to, and so on. Castes within Khalapur could be ranked rather exactly from these responses. Thus, it would appear that a local caste hierarchy is in considerable part a result of beliefs about pollution contagion and "ritual distance" (Mahar 1959; Marriott 1968b).

The caste system is a cooperative though not egalitarian system. Those who control food-producing land are at the center of the system. Thus, dominant caste households compose the most important jajmans.

William Wiser wrote a very detailed description of the intercaste exchange system of Karimpur, Mainpuri District, Uttar Pradesh (Wiser 1936). The term there for the client for whom servants and artisans worked was *jajmān*, a Hindi word coming from the Sanskrit *yajnya* meaning a sacrifice. The *yajmān* was the person upon whose behalf a Brahman performed a religious sacrifice. The term used in Khalapur was *jijmān*, a local version of the same word. Taken from the relationship between the Brahman household priest and his client and used in the context of other caste relationships, the word suggests a crucial feature of this system of exchange—that it is not purely economic, but is also a ritual system involving the concept of pollution, and duties connected with life cycle rites and other religious ceremonies.

Hocart, in describing a similar system in Ceylon, spoke of the specialists as "priesthoods." Gould, in particular, has emphasized the importance in the system of the lower castes' absorption of pollution on behalf of their jajmans (Gould 1958). In Khalapur, the servants saved their high caste jajmans from work deemed to be dirty (the Barber, Laundryman, Sweeper), or manual (Potter and Carpenter), or menial (Watercarrier), or work for which the Rajputs were not themselves pure enough (Brahman household priest). The employment of Sweeper and Watercarrier was connected with the seclusion of high caste women who were forbidden to go out to fetch water or to make dung-cakes for fuel. The concern with the purity of women is part of the pollution complex.

The jajmani system is widespread in India. Wherever it operates, the servants receive fixed payments in grain as their base wages. The servants believe themselves to have a *right* to support by their agriculturalist jajmans, who provide a part or sometimes all of the necessities required to live—various kinds of food, house sites, building materials, fuel, fodder, grazing land, use of tools and draft animals, credit facilities, and so on. The attitude of the landed jajman is ideally one of *noblesse oblige* and paternalism. The prestige of his social position is enhanced by having such retainers. And the retainers are, of course, important in contributing to the ostentatious displays at weddings, funerals, birth ceremonies, and other celebrations vital to the jajman's family reputation. Each servant has duties at these ceremonies.

Each high-caste jajman in Khalapur had six *lāgdārs* (servants)—a family each from the castes of Barbers, Watercarriers, Laundrymen, Carpenters, Potters, and Sweepers. The Brahman household priests, although they could not be called lagdars, also had a clientele of jajmans. There were other jatis which might once have had a regular clientele, but no longer had. These included Weavers, Shoemakers, and Oilpressers. The various mendicant jatis also included the Sectarian castes of *Jōgīs*, *Gosains*, and the *Sains*, as well as a jati of entertainers, the *Mirāsīs*.

A Sample Caste: The Sweepers of Khalapur. Let us look at the Sweepers of Khalapur as an example of a lagdar. Each team of Sweepers was usually composed of a pair of women who were mother and daughter, mother-in-law and daughter-in-law, or brothers' wives. Sometimes, if

necessary, men helped their wives, or some sons helped
their mothers; but clearly men tried to leave this jajmani work to women. The men preferred, if possible, to
find jobs in cities of the area. Each team of Sweepers
worked for an average of a dozen higher-caste households. The 188 households for which the Sweepers
worked in 1955 represented sixteen different castes.
Ninety-six were Rajputs, twenty were Brahman, eleven
were Carpenters, eleven were Oil-pressers, and there
were sprinklings of households (less than ten each)
from Merchants, Goldsmiths, Barbers, Watercarriers,
Tailors, Muslim Rajputs, Laundrymen, Gosains, Jogis,
Sains, and Untouchable Leatherworkers. The median six-
monthly income for each team was about 270 pounds of
grain. For each latrine in a jajman's house which a
team cleaned, it received one piece of new or good
women's clothing per year. In addition, the team received ten pounds of grain each six months for each
woman using a latrine in the jajman's house. Lastly,
the team got a piece of bread with vegetable or pulse
sauce every other day. For cleaning a cattleyard and
making dungcakes from the cattle droppings, they also
got twenty pounds of sugar per year, a new headbasket
as needed, and daily bread with vegetable or pulse
sauce. There were also optional services for which the
Sweeper team might be paid. At birth ceremonies, weddings, and funerals in the jajman's house, the Sweeper
lagdar family had a variety of duties for which the
group received payments and gifts.

The daily and ritual duties of the Sweepers and
other lagdars of Khalapur were so codified and well-
established that everyone knew them. Sweepers did not
always do their duties properly, and jajmans did not
always make the payments that they ought, but the
formulas for both duties and payments were consensually
validated even though quite highly detailed.

If a jajman was dissatisfied with his Sweepers'
work, he must complain to the headman of the Sweeper
jati-segment residing in the western section of Khalapur, especially if he wished to dismiss the Sweeper
team and to hire others. Only through the headman
could such a replacement be made. The headman would
consult with the elders and adult men. Similarly a
headman might talk to a jajman if the Sweepers had

cause for complaint. Any rash action on the part of a jajman might leave him boycotted with none of the Sweepers willing to work for him. New Sweepers could not easily be brought in without the Sweepers who were already in the village acting as sponsors. If there was too much work to do, then their relatives from less busy villages might be brought in to settle in the village.

Servants usually work for many jajmans, the number varying by their specialty. In Karimpur, studied by the Wisers, one florist served everyone in the village, while each Watercarrier served only three or four jajmans (Wiser and Wiser 1971). For Sherupur, Uttar Pradesh, studied by Gould, the number ranged from eleven jajmans each for the priest and plowman up to forty-three jajmans for the Washerman (Gould 1958: 436). The indispensability of a specialty also varies. A carpenter may be more vital than a supplier of betel leaves (used for chewing). A jati's job security depends upon its bargaining power which, in turn, depends upon the necessity of the service or product the jati members provide, the amount of competition members have from others willing to provide this service or product, as well as their own "union solidarity." The Sweepers had high bargaining power, and they had, from time to time, staged successful strikes when they felt they had been treated unfairly. The Watercarriers, in contrast, were in over-supply in the mid-1950s in Khalapur and probably would not have had success in a strike. Bargaining power and indispensability for a lagdar jati-segment living in a village or locality does not relate to ritual purity. Thus, the Untouchable Sweepers had higher bargaining power in Khalapur than did the middle-ranking ritually-clean Watercarriers.

Ideally, each jati has a monopoly on a particular service or product. Potters should not try to become Carpenters or *vice versa*. Relationships within the jajmani system are between families of two different castes. Thus, a Sweeper family has a relationship with a Rajput's family. The clientele of a pair of Sweepers should descend from one generation to the next within a family or minimal lineage. In fact, this was the case in Khalapur. A minimal lineage of Sweepers served a minimal lineage of Rajputs.

The jajmani relationships may become relevant to the factional politics so prevalent among members of a segment of a dominant caste in a locality. A servant may be expected to help his jajman in various ways to oppose another faction which might include other members of the servant's own jati. Thus, horizontal ties within a jati segment may be undermined by the vertical ties between families of different caste. Jajmans may also be drawn into disputes within the jati of a lagdar or into inter-jati disputes. Thus, in Khalapur, one lineage of Rajputs supported the Sweepers in a dispute with the Leatherworkers who, in turn, were supported by another lineage of Rajputs.

In some settings, the servants working for the same jajman may have especially close relations with each other, exchanging services or products (Rowe 1963: 42), or forming a well-coordinated production team (Barth 1960: 120-123).

THE DECLINE OF THE JAJMANI SYSTEM

The capability of a caste specialty to support the members of a jati varies with the demand for the products of the craft or the service in question. E. A. H. Blunt, writing on the caste system in the northern state of Uttar Pradesh, used the statistics from the 1911 Census of India and noted the variability among castes in the proportions of members following their caste occupation. He found that 76 percent or more of Sweepers and Goldsmiths; between 60 and 74 percent of Confectioners, Grainparchers, and Washermen; and 50 to 59 percent of Carpenters, Weavers, Oil-pressers, Barbers, and Potters were working at the specialty of their caste. In contrast, under 10 percent of Leatherworkers and Wine Dealers worked at their professions, and under 20 percent of Brahmans worked as priests. Blunt was of the opinion that the proportions of members of the caste not following their caste occupation (but working in agriculture, laboring, or acting as domestic servants) was due to a decline in the demand for handicrafts and traditional services. Agriculture has been permitted as an alternative occupation for all, but some castes have a traditional occupation of

cultivator. Blunt pointed out that 90 percent of those
in farming castes followed agriculture; but 43 percent
of those in non-agricultural castes were, nevertheless,
in agricultural work, as compared to 42.2 percent following their own original caste profession (Blunt 1931:
240-241).

The geographer, Joseph Schwartzberg, has also
shown the marked decline of craftsmen doing the kind of
work originally done by members of specialist castes.
Thus, in Khalapur, the Telis' traditional work was oil-
pressing, the Chamars' traditional work was leather
tanning, the Barber's wife and the Bharbhujas (grain
parchers) had done hand-grinding. Schwartzberg, using
data from the 1951 Census of India, shows that those
employed in "vegetable oil-pressing and refining" declined from 483,000 persons in 1901 to 250,000 persons
in 1951. A similar decline in the employment of "hand
pounding of rice, flour grinding, manual dehusking and
milling of cereals and pulses" was noted—from 1,245,
000 in 1901 to 526,000 in 1951. The number of "leather,
leather products, and footwear workers" declined from
1,143,000 in 1901 to 760,000 in 1951 (Schwartzberg
1963: 24).

Dumont suggests that the jajmani services have become restricted in modern times primarily to religious
and personal ones. Some specialties have disappeared
from the system entirely (Dumont 1970: 235).

The reasons for the decline in the jajmani system
are various. In Khalapur, the coming of the sugar
mills affected lagdars in a number of ways. The Rajput
landlords no longer pressed much sugarcane themselves,
so they gave out less home-produced unrefined sugar to
their servants; they also gave less of the waste scum
from sugar-making to the Sweepers' pigs. Affecting all
servants was the Rajputs' new tendency to plant a greater proportion of land in sugarcane and a smaller proportion in foodgrains. This meant that there was less
grain to give out in six-monthly payments, or in chari-
ties to begging low-caste women. In the largely non-
monetary, pre-market economy of the past, food produced
had to be consumed or it spoiled. So farmers readily
gave out surpluses to dependent landless people. In
Khalapur, with the introduction of sugarcane as the important cash crop, the jajmans were accused of changing,

from being generous to becoming greedy. Hard cash is not so liable to spoilage as is grain, and cash is what a landowner gets when he sells his cane to the mill.

In various other ways, the system was being undermined. The installation in the mid-1950s of handpumps for water within the courtyards of high-caste women's quarters made Watercarriers unnecessary. A sizeable *basti* (colony) of Watercarriers had already left Khalapur to go to the cities. The Potter's trade was undermined by the villagers' purchase and use of factory-made metal dishes and utensils, instead of the Potter's clay products. The availability of items such as shoes, shaves, and textiles in shops in market towns undermined the crafts of Shoemaker, Barber, and Weaver in the village. Some anthropologists report that villages are becoming depopulated as their contingents of artisan and servant castes leave for town (Karve and Randive 1965: 12; Mencher 1972: 51).

Occupational monopolies and inherited clienteles are no longer respected in some places (Berreman 1962; Mayer 1960). Jajmans are more ready to do the servants' work themselves, as did those jajmans in Rampur who began to shave themselves and do carpentry (Lewis 1958: 63, 67); or they ignored the requirement that they must hire and fire through the jati's elders, headmen, or caste council.

Joseph Elder has made one of the few studies which show what happens to those released from the past security of the jajmani system. (But see also Wiser 1971: 150, 189, 191, 192, 196, 247.) A calculation from Elder's figures from Rajpur, Uttar Pradesh, 1955, shows that out of 186 men in jatis previously employed in high numbers in jajmani relationships, only 7 worked full-time for jajmans—6 Carpenters and 1 Barber. Twelve Barbers, 2 Cotton-carders, and 2 Oil-pressers worked as jajmani servants part-time, presumably working as farmers the remaining time. Seventy-four previous jajmani servants now worked full-time as farmers; another 47 worked at the new sugar mill nearby; 6 worked for the railroad; 1 was waterman at the railroad station; 4 were tailors; 2 had set up carpenter shops near the sugar mill to rescue broken-down bullock carts carrying cane; 1 cleaned trucks; 21 were peddlers, mostly of various foods; 1 did grain-grinding; 5 were unemployed;

and for 6 there was no information. The Rajpur area is probably unusual in its capacity to provide former servants and artisans with land or agricultural work. In many villages, this alternative would not have been so readily available for so many. Even so, it is impressive to see how important the sugar mill, the railroad, and the sewing machine have become to the employment of these villagers. One-third have work because of these modern machines (Elder 1970).

INDENTURED AGRESTIC SERVANTS—THE HALI SYSTEM

A crucial feature of the caste system is the prohibition upon the twice-born against their plowing the earth. Possibly, this is part of the ideal of non-violence, seemingly absorbed into Hinduism from Jainism and Buddhism. The plow may kill living creatures as it cuts the furrows. In addition to this attitude, there is the devaluation of manual labor, especially of "filthy" tasks. Thus, where the dominant caste landholders are either Brahman or consider themselves to be Kshatriya (the second of the ancient varnas—the category of rulers and warriors), they depend upon lower castemen, usually Untouchable, to do the actual field labor. Thus, in many parts of India, the dominant caste is balanced at the other end of the caste hierarchy by a large landless caste of Untouchables (Dumont 1970: 161). This is true in rice-growing areas where large numbers of Untouchables do the highly-devalued back-breaking labor needed in paddy fields (Alexander 1975: 669).

In modern times agricultural laborers are not usually part of the jajmani system, but are paid monthly or seasonally in cash or kind. In the past, permanent relationships between a dominant caste family and a family of agrestic servants were common. The latter were called variously *harwahas, halis, kabadis,* or *adimais.* In pre-British times, the lot of some of these laborers could be described as slavery or serfdom, conditions abolished by British colonial law. While slavery entails one person's owning another, serfdom entails an individual bound to a piece of land, so that he or she is transferred with the land.

One of the largest castes in India is the Chamars of Northern India. As Untouchables, many still participate in local jajmani systems. They have the duty of taking away dead animals, the hides of which they tan, the bones of which they sell to traders who make bone-meal for fertilizer. In past centuries, the Chamars were said to have eaten the meat from the animals. Such dietary practice plus their association with dead animals made them a highly polluted caste. Many jatis of Chamars have given up both leather work and scavenging of dead animals. Thus, Mohinder Singh reported that only 7.6 percent of Chamars were doing such jajmani work in Uttar Pradesh in the 1940s, and only 5.7 percent were doing leather work (M. Singh 1947: 21, 80). They are known over Northern India as landless agricultural laborers (Briggs 1920).

Systems of serfdom, debt-bondage, forced labor, and permanent servitude seem to have disappeared very largely from India during the past century. This is one of the major ways in which the caste system has changed. There has been rather little study of such systems by anthropologists or historians (Beidelman 1959: 11). Fortunately, two recent studies by Edward Harper (1968a) and Jan Breman (1974) make it possible to understand the nature of such systems and to trace their decline.

A Study in a Havik Brahman Village. Edward Harper examined the gradual change in the status of the landless Untouchable Holerus in a Havik Brahman village in the upland Malnad area of Karnataka state (formerly Mysore). These people had long been dependent economically upon the cash crop of areca nuts. In the late eighteenth century, the Holerus were reported to have been in quasi-slavery, from which they were officially emancipated in the 1830s by the British rulers. Their condition, however, did not really change until the famine of 1876-78, during which the majority of "slaves" were freed. Subsequently they were involved in a system of lifelong indentureship. In recent decades, they have sought to establish new kinds of relationships between themselves and their high-ranking dominant caste members.

Under both the slavery system and the indenture system, the Brahman master financed his Holeru servant's marriage. Under slavery, however, a master could sell or rent out the slave, the slave's children belonged to the master, and the master had the right to punish his slave physically. The slave, on the other hand, had an occupational monopoly on plowing his master's fields. The Holeru servant lost this monopoly after the 1876-78 famine. At that time the middle-ranking caste of Divarus gave up their traditional occupation of toddy-tapping and soldiering and became more thoroughly established as agricultural tenants of the Havik Brahmans. However, control over the Holerus continued to be strong enough so that they were prohibited from owning land, or from taking up the traditional specialty of any other caste.

In the indentureship system, the servant was an employee of his master for life; and ideally his son inherited the relationship, continuing in the service of the employer's family. The relationship commenced with a contract initiated by the Holeru who wished to have his marriage financed by a Havik Brahman. The latter provided the food for the marriage feasts, money for the brideprice and bridal jewelry, and goods used for presents to wedding guests. Both husband and wife performed a milk-drinking ceremony, symbolizing their fealty to the Brahman family. Thenceforth, both husband and wife worked for the master's family—the man working in the areca nut garden, herding cattle, tending vegetables, and so on; the wife working in the Brahman household processing food grains, and occasionally helping out in gardens and fields. They were paid in amounts of paddy and other foodstuffs, occasional clothing and blankets, tobacco, kerosene, and small amounts of cash. The Holeru servant was expected to be loyal to his Brahman master, and the master and his family was expected to take a familistic interest in their servants.

In the mid-1950s, the system of lifelong indentureship was drifting toward a system of temporary indentureship. A number of changes were being tried. Holerus were refusing to go through the milk-drinking ceremony, considering it to be demeaning. Some tried to bargain for a higher payment in grain, and even to demand a monthly cash wage. They tried to have their wives relieved from service arrangements, and they tried to persuade the Havik Brahmans to limit the servitude to 15 or 20 years, rather than for life. Some Holerus managed to bargain for only part-time servitude, so that they might work as free wage-laborers the remaining time. At the time of marriage some signed promissory notes with interest specified and requested the master to pay only part of the paddy or cash coming to the servant seasonally, the rest being applied to amortize the debt.

Harper saw the Holerus as caught between their desire to marry in an elaborate and costly wedding, and their desire to be free, rather than indentured. The Holeru caste panchayat (council) had tried to lower brideprice without success, although some Holerus had lightened the brideprice burden by arranging less favored, but much cheaper exchange marriages (one in which each of two families gives a daughter in marriage to a son of the other). Many Holerus were not marrying at all, Harper said. Also, pre-marital pregnancies were occurring frequently with mandatory marriages following.

The most important factor in the situation described was the declining power of the Havik Brahmans themselves. Previously, they controlled the area politically, as well as economically. In the 1950s, government agencies, such as courts and political parties, which did not always support the Haviks, had cut into their power.

The system was breaking down in the 1950s. Of seventeen Havik Brahman families who had Holeru lifetime indentured servants, eight of those families had the servants quit their employment within the previous decade—breaking the contracts. Through Congress and Harijan (Untouchable) political parties, the Holerus had had contact with opinion decrying the indentureship system. As a result, they now looked upon indentureship as exploitation of the servant. The Haviks, in turn, were becoming increasingly reluctant to finance Holeru marriages—fearing that they would not get a return investment in the form of reliable labor. Recent legislation favored the low-caste, rather than the higher-caste master.

Previously the Havik Brahmans in the area cooperated with one another by not employing a runaway servant, and by seeing to it that a runaway was restored
to his master. Such Havik solidarity no longer exists,
while solidarity and caste consciousness among the Untouchables has increased. At the same time, prosperity
from areca nut sales has made the need for cheap labor
less pressing, and Haviks are more willing to employ
Holerus as wage laborers on more favorable terms of
payment. The government now ensures house sites for
Untouchables, so Haviks no longer have the power to
evict a wayward servant from his home, and courts are
much less biased. The Havik cannot count upon the
court to support the higher-caste plaintiff in a case
with a low-caste man. Tenantry legislation also pro-
tects the Holeru who was given a bit of land by his
master as part of the anchorage of indentureship.

The *Hali* System of Southern Gujarat. This system, described by Jan Breman (Breman 1974), is similar in many
features to the system of indentured servitude of the
Holerus, described by Harper. The word, *hali*, comes
from the word *hal*, meaning plow. Like the Holeru, the
hali was essentially a plowman, although he did any
other chore required by his high-caste master who was
called in Gujarat, a *dhaniamo*. As with the Holeru, the
hali's wife and children were also bound to the family
of the dominant caste family with which the hali
served. The hali's wife worked mainly in the dhaniamo's house—grinding grain, fetching water, sweeping,
emptying chamberpots, cleaning cattleyards—doing the
work often done by Untouchables elsewhere. And as with
the Holeru, one of the obligations of the master was to
provide for the expenses of the hali's marriage. Breman, however, emphasizes the fact that, according to
early Britisher's observations, neither the hali nor
his dhaniamo had any expectation that the debt would
ever be paid off. Furthermore, the hali's position was
not considered to be one of degradation, but rather one
of considerable security, since his master was obliged
to provide for all the needs of the hali and his family. The dhaniamo had first rights to the labor of the
son of his hali, since, it was said, the boy had grown
up on the dhaniamo's food. Thus, the relationship be-

tween the two families was often continued from generation to generation.

In the part of southern Gujarat where Breman did his field work, the dominant caste was Anavil Brahman, and the halis were mostly tribal Dublas. The Bhathela Anavils who lived in the villages Breman studied were very eager to emulate the higher-ranking Pedivala Desai section of their caste. These Desais had been royal representatives to the villages during the Moghul rule. The Desai landholders never did agricultural work themselves, but depended upon one or two halis. The Bhathelas similarly wanted land primarily as a status symbol and tried to employ halis, so that both men and women Bhathelas could be freed from field work for a life of conspicuous leisure. Thus, having halis was a matter of status and prestige, more than a matter of economic need. A man was judged by the number of servants he could provide for, not by the number he needed; they were retainers giving a man power in the village.

The dhaniamo was obliged to provide the hali family with daily food, clothing, a house site, the cost of materials for a hut, sometimes a bit of land to till, and tobacco, toddy, and spending money. The hali was expected to be perfectly loyal to his master, supporting him in any dispute. The exchange implicit in the relationship was the availability to the master of the servants' support, as well as a reliable labor supply during the peak seasons of harvest. For the hali, there was the security of being cared for in every way, albeit at a minimal level, by a landed family.

In the nineteenth century, the rural area of southern Gujarat was quite isolated, so there were few alternative employment opportunities for either Dublas or Anavils. A Dubla preferred to give his daughter in marriage to a Dubla who was a hali, rather than to one who was a free laborer, because of the economic security implied. In this system, the Anavil Brahmans were interested in maximizing power and prestige in the local area, not in maximizing profit from produce from the land.

The hali system is in an advanced state of decline today. There are a number of factors accounting for this. First, the power of the Anavils beyond the village in support of the system was reduced by the intrusion of British power. Officials of Anavil Brahman caste found that the British disapproved of the usual favoritism of an official for members of his own caste. Furthermore, the British were against the hali system, which they saw as a form of debt-bondage. Thus, under British rule, the Anavil dhaniamo could not look to the area officials to help him if a hali ran away. A second factor in the decline of the hali system was that while the population of the Anavil Brahmans increased 13 percent between 1881 and 1941, that of the Dublas increased 80 percent. Thus, the labor shortage at peak periods seems to have been partially relieved by the greater supply of potential laborers. Third, the Anavils began to raise mangoes rather than the labor-intensive crop of sugar cane. Mangoes need labor input only during the picking season. So the Anavils had a profitable crop requiring little labor and little supervision of labor. Previously, they had wanted continuous permanent labor, so that it would be available for the peak harvest season as well as for the care of sugar cane, ginger, spices, and other crops throughout the year. This labor supply became unnecessary with the crop change. Fourth, the means of transportation improved, so that the cities of Navsari, Surat, and Bombay were much more accessible from the villages. Now both Anavils and Dublas could seek work in the city. The Dublas began to go in the off-season to work in the salt-pans and brick-yards of Bombay. The Anavils sought jobs as clerks, officials, and teachers. Agricultural produce could also be more easily marketed. Fifth, the Anavils began to educate their sons to become white collar workers rather than landlords. The new generation Anavils emulated the style of life of the well-off in the city.

As a result of these factors, there was a new orientation. Previously, a large number of retainers meant enhanced prestige for an Anavil. Now, the new goal was to maximize profit from a cash crop. The dominant Anavils were much less concerned with having loyal retainers for political struggles or reasons of prestige. The relationship between them and their laborers was gradually commercialized, so that the landowner paid the wage necessary to attract labor to do specific jobs. Obligations to the laborer beyond payment for service rendered were increasingly ignored. Where permanent hali relationships were established, the relationship typically started at a much later age for the hali, and endured for a shorter period than before. As Harper has said, the indentureship becomes temporary rather than permanent. The Dublas themselves now preferred day labor to the hali role. An antagonism between Anavils and Dublas had replaced an earlier mutuality. Some Anavils began to use tractors in place of laborers in part to avoid the problems of dealing with Dubla subordinates. New forms of labor relationships developed, including a piecework system whereby a labor-gang agreed to harvest a field or do some other task for a prearranged price. Also, some Anavils employed seasonal migratory laborers who come into southern Gujarat from western Maharashtra.

The condition of the Dublas deteriorated. Their living sites were more crowded. Previously it had been the right of servants to take a portion of whatever the master produced on his land. Under the new system, this right ceased to exist. Landowners fenced their property with barbed wire to prevent pilfering of wood or crops.

Political actions have not helped the Dublas much. The Gandhian campaign with the *Hali Sevak Sangh*, a hali emancipation movement, has made halis more conscious of their exploited condition, but has not improved their economic condition. State-level minimal wage legislation for farm workers has been generally ignored, since the law was not enforced. A land grab movement by the halis in 1970 failed; many Dublas and lower-caste people were jailed. Breman refers to a process of *pauperization* of the Dublas, both in rural or urban areas, for industry in the region has not developed sufficiently to absorb the new rural proletariat.

Chapter 4

The Caste System Analyzed: The Ideology of Purity and Pollution

Caste, found universally in Hindu India, has been a key institution integrating the culture. The institution of caste is composed of certain universal Hindu ideas. These include the Hindu pollution concept; the social units of *jatis* (endogamous large-scale descent-groups); the cognitive categories of *varnas* (ranked classification of jatis); the associated concepts of *jatidharma* (religiously-given duties for jati members) and *varnadharma* (religiously-given duties for varna members); and the inter-jati local division of labor, such as the *jajmani* system, which makes a *system* of a multiplicity of bounded social units within a village or set of neighboring villages. In this chapter, the ideology of purity and pollution is considered.

HINDU PURITY-IMPURITY

The principle of purity-impurity pervades and partly explains the hierarchy of castes. Gods, people, social groups (jatis and minimal patrilineages), animals, and things may be ranked in a hierarchy of degrees of purity and impurity. Each member of each of these categories possesses, as an individual *attribute*, some capacity to pollute others. Each, however, may become more polluted, either temporarily or permanently, through *transactions* with *more* polluted beings, things, or happenings. Indeed, such transactions *display* the relative rankings of beings and items in a hierarchy of degrees of purity-impurity. This principle may be understood through the underlying Hindu imagery relating to living and dead organisms.

In recent decades a number of anthropologists have contributed to a theory of Hindu purity-impurity. These include A. M. Hocart (1950); M. N. Srinivas (1952); H. N. C. Stevenson (1954); Harold Gould (1958); Pauline Mahar (Kolenda) (1959); Nur Yalman (1963); Edward Harper (1964); Henry Orenstein (1970); Louis Dumont (1970, 1959); McKim Marriott and Ronald Inden (1973, 1977); and Marvin Davis (1976). These scholars' part-theories are not contradictory so much as complementary. Each usually has integrated his or her predecessors' ideas into his or her own.

Priestly-Purity Necessary for Transactions with the Gods. A central point in Hindu ritual is that it is necessary to make offerings to the gods in order for human affairs to continue without undue disaster. The intermediary between the general society and the gods is the priest, typically a Brahman. The Brahman priest must be pure in order to communicate with the gods, and satisfactory communication with the supernatural powers is necessary for the good of the king and of the society. This idea goes back to the ancient Aryan idea of *Rita* (order), the belief that the sacrificial offerings made by Brahmans were a necessary part of the natural order. If such offerings were not made, or if they were not made correctly, then nature would go awry—rain would not fall, epidemics might prevail, and so on (Basham 1954: 113, 236-237). It was, thus, vital for the Brahmans to be pure. As A. M. Hocart saw clearly with respect to caste-ordered ritual in Ceylon, the function of lower castes was to absorb pollution for the higher castes (Hocart 1950). In India, too, the lower castes absorb pollution for the Brahman and for the other "twice-born" (Gould 1958; Dumont 1970: 55).

Both M. N. Srinivas (1952: 101-122) and Edward Harper (1964: 152-155) have specified three conditions of pollution and purity for Mysore villagers—a state of normal purity, a state of impurity, and a state of ritual purity. In the latter condition, one might transact with divinities, namely gods and ancestors. Means of purification include taking a bath and wearing pure clothes. There are many agents causing states of impurity. Contact with lower-caste persons is only one such agent. Others include contact with death, birth, menstruation, sexual intercourse, defecation, urination, bodily dirt, and eating.

STEVENSON'S "HINDU POLLUTION CONCEPT"

H. N. C. Stevenson delineated the underlying principle of pollution. Basically, any waste product from a human, animal, or divine body is impure. With death, the entire body becomes waste. A Brahman priest, in preparation for his religious service, purifies himself from the pollution of his own body, as well as from any pollution acquired by contact with polluted persons or places. Thus a Brahman *tantri* (officiant in a temple) today remains continent, fasts, bathes, and wears a clean waist cloth before appearing before the god in the temple. A tantri's purity can be only temporary, because he will soon have to defile himself by eating, defecating, and so on. If a member of his family or patrilineage should die, or if a wife of one of the male members has a child, the tantri cannot appear in the temple for many days. He is assumed to be polluted by the birth or death pollution pervading his family or patrilineage (it pervades male relatives and their wives in a patriline up to second cousin) (*Travancore Devaswom Manual* Vol. I:166, 182, 184).

Dietary and Marital Customs. Besides pollution from a caste's traditional occupation, its dietary and marital customs are relevant to its ritual rank. Absorbed into Hinduism from Buddhism and Jainism was a belief in non-violence; and, consequently, a belief that a vegetarian diet characterizes the purer castes. There are, furthermore, degrees of non-vegetarianism. It is especially defiling to eat the meat of the sacred cow. The next worst is eating pork, then mutton, then chicken, then fish, then eggs. Consistent with this, Brahmans are usually vegetarian; middle castes may eat chicken or

The Ideology of Purity and Pollution 65

mutton; and Untouchables may eat these plus pork or beef, as well.

To be pure, a high caste woman should have only a single sexual partner throughout her life. Those castes which allow a woman to marry only once are considered to be higher than those which allow widow remarriage, or which allow women to divorce and remarry. When a Brahman jati is said to have *no divorce*, what is meant is that a woman is not allowed to have a second husband. Men, whether Brahmans or of other castes, are allowed to have more than one wife. Even as his first wife is virginal, so a Brahman's second or subsequent wives are virginal upon marriage. Of course, in many middle and lower castes, widow remarriage is allowed. Sometimes women are allowed to divorce and remarry, but this is one of the customs which keeps them in a low rank in the caste hierarchy.

Pollution Inherited by Caste. The tantri's impurity is also temporary; by various cleansing action, he can become pure again. For lower castes, impurity is permanent. Lower caste members suffer a kind of inherited defilement. The Barber deals with bodily wastes—hair and nail clippings; he washes the male corpses, and his wife washes the female corpses of his higher caste *jajmans* (clients). The Washerman washes dirty clothing, stained by bodily excretions. The Sweeper removes human filth; he eats from pots spoiled by birth and death pollution pervading a jajman's house; he wears clothing in which a jajman died; he eats left-over food that has touched the mouths of others, or meat from dead animals. So degrees of defilement relate to the ranks in a caste hierarchy. The Barber is less defiled than the Washerman, who, in turn, is less defiled than the Sweeper, and so on.

The idea of pollution-contagion is universal in Hindu India. Anything touched by a polluted person spreads the pollution to others who touch it. This notion is expressed in rules about giving food and water, and touching persons and their belongings. An orthodox Brahman will not take boiled food or water from anyone of lower caste rank. He may take food coated by purifying milk or *ghi* (clarified butter), products of the sacred cow, from professional confectioners, and from some other persons of somewhat lower caste rank. Since fire purifies, he may take from almost anyone raw ingredients which will be purified in the process of cooking.

DUMONT'S PURITY-IMPURITY PRINCIPLE

Louis Dumont's book, *Homo Hierarchicus*, is a major theoretical work on the caste system. The underlying principle of this hierarchy is purity-impurity. Following Stevenson, Dumont defines impurity as "the irruption of the biological into social life." Hindus are temporarily impure when in contact with twelve polluting secretions of the body (Dumont 1970: 61, 49). Castes are separate, but interdependent hereditary groups of occupational specialists. It is the principle of purity-impurity which operates to keep the segments separate from one another. Each jati closes its boundaries to lower jatis, refusing them the privilege of intermarriage and other contacts defined as polluting to the higher jati. Each jati, in turn, is excluded by the jatis ranking above it in a local caste hierarchy. Thus, differences in degree of pollution create closed segments, as each segment tries to preserve its own degree of purity from contamination by lower castes. It is, in turn, excluded as a contaminator by castes above (Dumont 1970: 59-60, 197).

Biological Substantialism: The Dividual-Particle Theory of Pollution. Dumont's, Stevenson's, Srinivas', and Harper's method of analysis involves the specification of the principles relating to agents and states of impurity and purity. It is not clear in their analyses whether the principles they specify are clearly articulated by native informants or not. Since the three states of purity and impurity mentioned by Harper and Srinivas have names in the Mysorean informants' languages, we may be fairly sure that these stages are recognized by the informants themselves. This is not so clear for Stevenson's principles of internal and external, temporary and permanent pollution. It is also not clear whether native informants could articulate Dumont's point that a principle of purity-impurity results in boundedness, the closure of jati units; or whether the point made by Hocart and Gould that lower castes "absorb the pollution" of upper castes is articulated or recognized by their Hindu informants. The issue of the natives' understandings, or cognitive view of their own societies was not ascendant in anthropology at the time these scholars were writing in the 1950s and 1960s. Most scholars did not address that issue. In the 1970s, however, the issue of "emic" versus "etic" conceptualizations has been in the forefront of social-cultural anthropology.

The contrast between "emic" and "etic" has been borrowed from linguistics (Pike 1967: 27-39). In linguistics the term phonemes refers to the minimal sounds in a language recognized by the native speakers themselves. In contrast, *phonetics* refers to the minimal sounds in the language recognized by trained linguistic anthropologists as they record the sounds in a general linguistic system of notation. These terms are now applied to other aspects of a culture besides language. An "emic" analysis gives the insider's, the native's interpretation or "model" of some cultural phenomena; an "etic" analysis gives the outsider's, the anthropologist's interpretation or "model."

McKim Marriott, an anthropologist, and Ronald B. Inden, a historian well-versed in Bengali and Sanskrit, have tried to characterize the "emic" view—the natives' "model" of the Hindu caste system (1973, 1977). Their "ethnosociology of the caste system" takes major account of what others, such as Stevenson, have considered as the "Hindu pollution concept" but treats this concept as part of what Hindus believe about physics, biology, and sociology. Specifically, their view takes up the human bodily contribution to social processes. It can answer such questions as: What is it that actually defiles water for a higher-caste person when it comes from the hands of an Untouchable? What is it about the semen of a higher-caste man that does not pollute a lower-caste female sexual partner?

The Indian anthropologist, Sarat Chandra Roy, suggested some decades ago that lower caste persons may once have been thought to have possessed some invisible power such as the powers of *mana* and *tabu* believed in by Oceanic peoples (Roy 1934, 1937, 1938; Hutton 1963:

182, 187-188). Radcliffe-Brown (1950: 139), inspired by Émile Durkheim (1915), and followed by M. N. Srinivas (1952), suggested that ritual power was projected into objects by the attribution of holiness or uncleanliness in people themselves. Thus the sacredness of objects was a projection of a people's reverent attitude. Marriott and Inden would object to these as "etic" explanations of the human contribution to pollution processes (although they do not actually use the terms "emic" and "etic"); these theories come out of anthropology's store of ideas, not out of the minds of native Hindus. Their own explanation aims to be "emic"; it is an attempt to state the sociology of the natives themselves, a Hindu "ethnosociology."

Marriott and Inden draw their understanding not only from the ethnography of everyday avoidances and exchanges, but from Hindu writings, including the Vedas, which concern sacrificial worship, from Brahmans, Upanishads, from classical books of moral and medical sciences, and from late medieval moral code books of certain castes in Bengal. They do not consider these texts to be ethnographic; that is, accurate descriptions of Hindus' actual behavior in olden times. But they do not treat them merely as records of the "ideal culture," either. These writings are sometimes seen by outsiders as "prescriptive"—as giving principles for behavior—but Marriott and Inden see in them more than that. They see them as records of the cognitive concepts, the ways of thinking of reflective, educated Hindus. Hindu native models today may be derived from such writings. By using such sources, Marriott and Inden claim to have found some ways in which Hindus themselves understand caste processes.

What they find is this: Unlike Westerners who think in terms of a duality of separable body and spirit, or body and mind, Hindus think monistically. Hindus believe that a person inherits a *unitary coded-substance*. The code "programmed" into the person's substance or body relates to his or her varna, jati, sex, and personality.

With respect to *varnadharma*, the code for members of each of the four *varnas* (priests, warrior-rulers, herdsmen-agriculturalists, servants), Marriott and Inden explain the sacrificial superman found in the Rig

Veda (see page 30, Cultures Combined: Hinduism). He is
a "Code Man" from which the "genera" (varnas) of human
beings were derived. Each genus (varna) is believed to
have received its particular code from a different part
of the body of the "Code Man."

Similarly, one's *jatidharma*, the duty of one's
jati, is encoded into one's bodily substance, as are
the duties for one's sex and personality. Such a code
does not determine exact behavior, however, but represents "internal formulae for uplifting conduct," pre-
scriptions for what one knows one should do as *natural-
ly* appropriate for one's own kind of person.

There are features of the coded-substance that explain the process of pollution. First of all, this
coded-substance is made up of coded-particles (in Sanskrit, *piṇḍas* and other terms). These particles—bits
of hair, sweat, saliva, etc.—may be shared or exchanged with others, and it is such particles that mix
into food, water, and other things transferred in interpersonal transactions. Thus, one gives off coded-
particles and gains coded-particles from others. One
should try to gain suitable or better coded-particles
(those coming from gods or higher castes), not worse
coded particles (those coming from lower castes or defiled persons) than one's own. One may get better
particles through "right eating, right marriage, and
other right exchanges and actions" (Marriott and Inden
1977: 233). One may rid oneself of inferior particles
through disposal as in excretion, or other processes
"often aided by persons of suitably lower genera." As
understood by Hocart and Gould, lower caste persons absorb pollution, here specified as inferior coded-
particles, from higher caste persons.

A second important feature of a coded-substance is
that its parts or particles can be loosened to separate
and combine with other kinds of coded-substance. Marriott and Inden explain:

> Heat is catalytic in many of these internal proc-
> esses and external exchanges: it creates an in-
> stability that facilitates either separation or
> combination among particles of different kinds of
> substance. Processes like digestion and sexual
> intercourse require heat to separate, to distill,

and to mix different substances. You are always likely to become what you eat, and you may also be atomically involved in what you feed to others, but especially so if and when the food is hot. Hence cooking and the serving and eating of warm foods like boiled rice and ordinary fresh, unleavened bread are liminal processes in which bodily and nutritive substances must be very carefully managed.

(Marriott and Inden 1977: 233)

This theory of coded-substances which are inherited, and which break up into coded-particles, especially through the catalyst of heat, to recombine with other kinds of particles, offers a theory of pollution-contagion. Presumably some of the coded-particles of the lower caste person's coded-substance is actually transferred to the higher caste person, through food, water, touch, or contact with the lower caste person's bodily products. Such a theory may strike a western reader as strange. It is a theory, however, which is to be found in the revered writings of Hindus themselves, and thus represents the native point of view, according to Marriott and Inden.

Marriott and Inden say that the instability of the coded-substance of the person, its ready break-up into particles, shows that the Hindu view of the person is of a one that is "dividual," a one which divides up into separable portions. Such a "dividual" image contrasts with the Western image of the person as an "individual," these authors say. They also assert that the monistic Hindu view which does not separate substance from code—i.e., body from morality—marks it as very different from Westerners' typically dualistic mode of thinking. Because of the instability of a person's coded-substance, the Hindu person must strive to maintain his appropriate coded-substance and possibly better it, not just avoid pollution, Marriott and Inden claim. ". . . the players have at stake also the preservation and transformation of their own natures." (Marriott 1976: 112)

THE GUN THEORY OF POLLUTION

Marriott and Inden's student, Marvin Davis (1976), has gone on to explain the nature of "coded-substance" from the viewpoint of Hindus of West Bengal. Davis learned of this folk-theory largely from interviewing Bengali Hindus, but the theory is drawn from Hindu holy books, including the *Bhagavad Gita*, and *Srimad Bhagavata Mahapurana*, the *Purusukta*, and the *Manu Dharmasastra*. Since these works are known widely in India, we may expect to find this theory held in other areas besides West Bengal. Davis' "emic" explanation, the Hindus' own cognitive model, enlarges the simpler "etic" models which represent the outsider's views in Stevenson's and Dumont's analyses. Davis' "emic" explanation connects with philosophical Hinduism as Stevenson's and Dumont's do not. It is not primarily a theory of pollution, but it does incidentally explain pollution and purity.

Here is an outline of this folk model:
All beings and things in the Hindu cosmos are made out of one substance, a female substance called *prakrti*. This basic material becomes differentiated into three substances by the joining of the female *prakrti* with male matter, *purusa*. Thus, a female natural *substance* joins with a male cultural principle, or *code*. So it is that prakrti and purusa make up what Marriott and Inden have called coded-substance.

The three basic materials (*guns*) formed by the union of *prakrti* and *purusa* are *sattvagun*, *rajogun*, and *tamogun*. Sattvagun, a white substance, "generates goodness and joy and inspires all noble virtues and actions." Rajogun, red, "produces egoism, selfishness, violence, jealousy, and ambition." Tamogun, black, "engenders stupidity, laziness, fear, and all sorts of base behavior." (Davis 1976): 9) Differing beings and phenomena have differing proportions of the three coded-substances.

The hierarchy of beings is composed of Brahma, the creator, at the top, followed by the gods, then humans, then demons, animals, plants, and minerals at the bottom. In Brahma, the three guns are present and in balance. In other beings, one or the other gun predominates. The gods are largely sattvagun. Among men,

the four varnas differ. The Brahmans are largely sattvagun. The Kshatriyas are largely rajogun, and the
Shudras and Untouchables are largely tamogun. Demons
and animals are largely rajogun, while plants and minerals are largely tamogun.

This native theory is close to Stevenson's Hindu
Pollution concept and Dumont's principle of purity-
impurity, since sattva may be translated as purity, and
tamogun as impurity. Sattvagun and tamogun, however,
imply considerably more than just purity and impurity.
How does rajogun come in? It is a "material mode that
activates the other two gun." (Davis 1976: 9)

Foods related to the three guns. "Cool food"
(milk, clarified butter, most fruits, and vegetables)
make sattvagun. "Hot foods" (meat, eggs, onions, mangoes) make rajogun. Spoiled or stale food make tamogun, as do beef and alcohol. Food from the gods,
prasad, is fraught with sattva; so it is beneficial to
eat food which has been placed before, and hence tasted
of, by the gods. The left-over food of the gods then
makes sattvagun. The left-over food of humans makes
tamogun, except when left-over food of very high caste
persons is eaten by very low-caste persons, when, presumably, it also makes sattvagun. (Davis 1976: 21).

What Stevenson called "permanent pollution" may be
understood in this theory as admixtures of the guns in
a jati, with tamogun in sizeable proportion. The differing proportion of the guns in different jatis relates to caste diet, work and life-styles, marriage
patterns, and inter-caste transactions. Different
castes have different diets. Vegetarian castes would
be more sattvagun; non-vegetarian, more rajogun. Those
which drink alcohol and eat beef, and left-over and
spoiled food would be more tamogun. The work of Brahmans makes sattvagun; that of scavengers, tanners,
prostitutes, work connected with the animal impulses of
humans, makes tamogun. Occupations that maintain life
in the ordinary world such as agriculturalists, herders,
artisans, and traders makes rajogun in their adherents.

According to this theory, Davis agrees with Marriott and Inden that persons and jatis do not have
fixed coded-substances. Both persons and jatis may
strive to improve their coded-substances, their admixtures of guns, by eating sattvik foods and doing satt-

vik work such as religious ritual, meditation, and learning. Similarly, they should try through marriage to maintain or improve the coded-substance of person and jati.

Davis relates the Bengali Hindus' theory of human conception. Food changes into digested food, which changes into blood, which changes into flesh, which changes into fat, which changes into marrow from which are derived semen in the male, and uterine blood in the female (Davis 1976: 19). In the conception of a child, the semen of the male and the uterine blood of the female unite. Intra-caste endogamy can be understood as a practice ensuring that these uniting components in conception will transmit to a child blood of equal gun-composition from both parents. As Marriott has put it:

> The offspring are ranked so that genera origi-
> nating from more homogeneous ancestry and from
> more consistent or harmonic (sexually and occu-
> pationally) acts of mixture stand higher.
>
> (Marriott 1976: 114)

Particles of inferior coded-substance, rajogun or tamogun, may be transferred with boiled food, raw un-cooked food (from the hands of Untouchables), or with drinking water. It is less easily transferred through food cooked in the cooling ghi which seems to make food fried in ghi (clarified butter) productive of sattva-gun. So a higher caste individual might take food cooked in ghi from the hands of a lower caste person, from whom he would not accept boiled rice or drinking water. Since heat tends to purify food, the higher caste person might take raw uncooked food from all but the lowly Untouchable.

The actions which improve one's coded-substance can, through concerted change in habits, raise the coded-substance of the whole caste. Davis explains:

> Through activities in accord with *dharma* and
> through mixing one's own physical nature with that
> of *sattvik* substances, for example, the defining
> features of a birth-group are transformed posi-
> tively and its rank elevated; for in this way
> individuals of the group and the birth-group as a

whole become more cognizant of Brahma and lead a more uplifting, spiritual life.

(Davis 1976: 16)

RANKING CASTES BY RULES OF POLLUTION-CONTAGION

The castes in village Khalapur may be ranked by the criterion of pollution-contagion. In 1955, eighteen villagers of nine different castes were asked about the ritual interactions they would permit themselves to have with twenty-one other castes. Could the person of the other caste touch one's children? Could he or she touch the informant? Would one take dry food from the person of the other caste? Would one take *pakka* food (cooked in *ghi*) from the person of the other caste? Would one take *kachcha* (boiled) food from the person of the other caste? Could such a person smoke the bowl of one's pipe? Would he or she touch one's brass utensils? one's earthenware vessels? one's water vessel? one's cot? Could the person of the other caste come into one's cooking area?

It was found that these ritual gestures, ones which would involve pollution-contagion, were regularly ordered by the Khalapur respondents by degrees of seriousness of the pollution transmitted. Most serious was the transfer of boiled food, or touching a water vessel, coming into a cooking area, or touching one's earthenware vessel. Least serious was the transfer of dry food, or touching one's children. Food cooked in water is considered to be more easily contaminated than is food protected by being cooked in *ghi* (clarified butter, product of the sacred cow). Water is also readily contaminated. The cooking area must be kept pure, because all food is prepared there. Porous earthenware vessels used for boiling food are more easily polluted than brass vessels which are used for frying or baking, the hardness of which can be cleaned by ashes. (See figures 4.1-4.4.) Respondents would allow more castes to perform the less polluting actions with respect to themselves than would allow the more polluting actions.

The number of other castes allowed to perform each action varied according to the respondent's own

Figure 4.1

Ritual Purity Continuum of Six Items

Score 0	1	2	3	4	5	6
	13 touch children	1 touch you	7 smoke bowl of pipe	4 touch brass utensils	8 accept fried (pakka) food	9 accept boiled (Kachcha) food
	10 dry food	2 cot				12 water vessel
						3 cooking area
						5 earthenware vessels

(Mahar 1959: 139)

Figure 4.2

Scoring from Six Items of the Purity-Pollution
Continuum

Score	Items					
0	---					
1	13					
2	13	1				
3	13	1	7			
4	13	1	7	4		
5	13	1	7	4	8	
6	13	1	7	4	8	9

(Mahar 1959: 139)

Figure 4.3

Scale-Picture of Responses Indicating Ritual Distance For Manbhi, Brahman Caste, Female, 40.

Items: **	Can touch our children (13)	Can accept dry, uncooked food (10)	Can touch me (1)	Can sit on our cot (2)	Can smoke bowl of pipe (7)	Can take water from his hand (11)	Can touch our brass vessels (4)	Can accept fried (Pakka) food from him (8)	Can smoke our pipe (6)	Can accept boiled (Kachcha) food from his hand (9)	Can touch our water vessel (12)	Can come on our cooking area (3)	Can touch our earthenware vessels (5)	Score
CASTES:														
Rajput	X	X	X	X	X	X	X	X	X	X	X			10
Merchant	X	X	X	X	X	X	X	X	X	X				10
Water-carrier	X	X	X	X	X	X	X	X	X	[O]				10-11
Goldsmith	X	X	X	X	X	X	X	X	X					9
Genealogist	X	X	X	X	X	X	X	X	X					9
Barber	X	X	X	X	X	X	X	X						8
Gosain	X	X	X	X	X	X								6
Shepherd	X	X	X	X	X	X								6
Carpenter	X	X	X	X	[O]	X								6
Potter	X	X	X	X	X	X								5-6
Washerman	X	[O]	X	X	X	X								5
Grainparcher	X	[O]	X	X	X	X								5
K. P. Weaver	X	X	X	X	X									3-4
Jogi	X	X	X	X	X									3-4
Mus. Rajput	X	O	X	X	X									3
Oilpresser	X		X	X										2
Mirasi	X		[X]											1-2-3
Ch. Weaver														0
Shoemaker														0
Chamar														0
Sweeper														0

No. Deviant Responses : 5
Total Responses : 273

(Mahar 1959: 133)

Figure 4.4

Scorings of Castes Derived from Manbhi's Scale-Picture
(Figure 4.3)

Score

10	Rajput, Merchant, Water-carrier
8	Genealogist, Goldsmith, Barber
6	Gosain, Shepherd, Carpenter, Potter
5	Washerman, Grainparcher
4	Jogi, Kabir Panthi Weaver
3	Muslim Rajput
2	Oilpresser, Mirasi
0	Chamar Weaver, Shoemaker, Chamar Sweeper

(Mahar 1959: 137)

Drawing of Namburi Brahmans of Travancore (from Samuel
Mateer, *The People of Travancore, Their Manners and
Customs.*   London: John Snow, 1871, p. 30.)

rank. A Brahman respondent would allow very few other castes to perform the more seriously polluting actions, while a lower caste person, such as a Potter, would allow more other castes to perform the more seriously polluting actions. Furthermore, all respondents tended to allow actions involving pollution to other castes in much the same order. If a Brahman would take kachcha food from a person from any other caste, it would be from a Rajput or Merchant. A Potter woman, of lower caste rank than the Brahman, would take *kachcha* food from Rajput and Merchant, but also from the Goldsmith and Carpenter.

From the responses of eighteen persons of nine different castes, a ranking of fifteen castes emerged with the Brahman at the top followed by representatives of the Kshatriya and Vaisya varnas locally, the Rajputs and Merchants, with the Untouchable Shoemakers, Chamars, and Sweepers at the bottom. The ranking of fifteen castes for Khalapur was this:

1 Brahman
2 Rajput
3 Merchant
4 Goldsmith
5 Genealogist
6 Barber
7 Water-carrier
8 Grainparcher
9 Shepherd
10 Muslim Rajput
11 Oilpresser
12 Beggar
13 Shoemaker
14 Chamar
15 Sweeper

(Mahar 1959)

A number of subsequent studies affirmed the relationship between pollution-contagion and caste ranking (Mayer 1960; Marriott, Freed, and Nicholas 1967; Marriott 1968; Beck 1972). What has become increasingly clear, however, is that pollution-contagion is not the only basis for caste ranking in a locality. H. N. C. Stevenson referred to *secular* criteria of stratification, especially economic and political power of

various kinds. This stratification may well be re-
flected in what might appear to be a hierarchy based on
the Hindu Pollution Concept (Stevenson 1954: 63).
  Louis Dumont who emphasized the purity-impurity
principle as the basis of hierarchy in the caste system
was, nevertheless, troubled by the high ranking (usually just below the highest ranking Brahmans) of the
Kshatriya-style dominant castes whose life-style was
often quite impure. They usually eat meat and drink
liquor, and as warriors indulge in violence, at least
in the past, as did the Rajputs of Khalapur. Their
diet and occupation might be considerably less pure
than those of castes ranked below them such as the
Vaishya Merchants. As in Khalapur, the Merchants are
strict vegetarians, and follow a peaceful non-violent
occupation of shopkeeping or trading.
  To solve this inconsistency in ranking castes by
purity-impurity alone, Dumont turned to the writings of
the ancient Hindus concerning the four varnas. Here he
found a clear subordination of the king (Kshatriya) to
the priest (Brahman). The religious principle, the
principle of purity, was given highest priority, as indicated by the highest rank being given to the Brahman
priest. However, for the king to perform his duty,
which was to rule, he had to have high status; otherwise the king's dignity, his usefulness, would be
denied (Dumont 1970: 77). So the king and, analogously,
the local kshatriya-style dominant castes, receive rank
just below the Brahman priest, even though they may be
more impure (or more rajogun than sattvagun) than the
Vaishya who are in rank below them.
  While Dumont rather lamely explains the high rank
of the dominant caste or kings by introducing the requirement that they be respected by their subjects—
they must be dignified—he does not take up the problem
of ranking lower castes which do not seem to have anything to do with removing pollution from the higher
castes. How is the rank of certain artisans determined?
Why in Khalapur does the Goldsmith have higher rank
than the Grainparcher? Neither seems to function as a
remover of pollution for higher castes. The greater
skill of the Goldsmith and the preciousness of gold
perhaps account for his higher rank.

McKim Marriott has suggested that other principles besides purity and pollution are operating as criteria in ranking castes. The giver of food is always ranked higher than the receiver. To reverse this statement, the served is ranked higher than the servant who is paid in food.

Marriott notes that the work of many castes in Kishan Garhi, Uttar Pradesh does not involve the removal of pollution. The work of Carpenters, Gardeners, Jogi devotees, Watermen, Cottoncarders is:

> . . . explicitly intended to exalt the master and his caste, not by avoiding or subtracting negative qualities, but by adding proof of his honor, religious merit, liberality, or power.
>
> (Marriott 1968: 144-145)

Servants are usually paid in the currency of foods and grain, so food transactions reflect the social relationship of served and servant. Marriott suggests that the food most readily accepted in intercaste transactions are also the most expensive and preferred foods. *Kachcha* food (boiled food) is considered to be inferior and less preferred because it lacks the very much preferred *ghi* (clarified butter). *Pakka* food, made with ghi, is superior food . . .

> the only kind of meal which can be offered in feasts to gods, to guests of high affinal status, to those who provide honorific services, and generally to persons of other castes . . . Ghee (clarified butter) is the costliest of the fats known locally.
>
> (Marriott 1968: 144)

Left-over food and feces can be understood not only as polluted substances, so that those having to remove them are polluted, Untouchable, but also as materials of "small monetary and nutritional worth." Their removal indicates the "extremity of domination" of the servant by the served (Marriott 1968: 144).

Raw foods which are readily accepted by high castes from lower castes often include highly preferred, costly foods such as wheat flour, sugar, ghi, and fruit. Unground grain may be preferred, because it can be used readily as a currency in a variety of subsequent transactions (Marriott 1968: 143).

Marriott concludes that the heart of the system of caste rank is serving and being served, not purity-impurity. The end result is the maintenance of a certain kingly style of life which the dominant caste particularly tries to enjoy, and which other castes may also emulate. In Kishan Garhi, in fact, an action may be defined as polluting in some contexts, but not polluting in others. The key is the maintenance of the subordination of the servant to the served. Marriott says:

> Thus with foods, although persons of castes above the lowest two refuse to accept food in any form, not even in the pure form of whole grain, from a Sweeper as gift or payment, they will nevertheless accept grain which was actually harvested or threshed by a Sweeper if he worked as an employee under a landowner of a caste higher in rank. Not the substance, of the Sweeper's touch, but his rank in the transaction is what matters. Similarly, flour ground by a Leatherworker woman in her own house and sold or given away by her is regarded as inedible by Brahmans, while flour ground by her working as an employee in a Brahman house is quite acceptable to the same consumers. Not touch or house, but control of the work defines purity or pollution in this case. . . . Obviously the maintenance of rank, not pollution by proximity, is the issue on which action turns in such instances . . . If there is one master conception on which village thinking about caste rank constantly focuses, this appeared to me to be the idea of the intercaste transaction. In their transactions with each other caste, the members of a caste take either higher rank through giving or commanding, or lower rank through receiving or serving.
>
> (Marriott 1968: 145-146)

Marriott has gone on to claim that Indian society is highly transactional (Marriott 1976). With respect to caste, the giver is of superior rank to the receiver, and the served is superior to the server. This exchange of service for gifts of food and other goods seems to be at the heart of the caste system, and is, of course, at the heart of the *jajmani* system, described in Chapter 3. A serving caste's capacity to pollute is presumably adjusted to the degree of servitude. Marriott says:

> . . . the castes in an Indian village . . . are partly scored by indigenous opinion, and are ascribed natures, qualities, ranks, and powers that correspond to the castes' relative dominance in the normal round-robin of transactions in substance-code, such as foods.
> (Marriott 1976: 111)

Castes can be ranked by the balance between the inter-caste transactional contexts in which a caste is a *giver* and those in which a caste is a *receiver* of foods and other gifts. While other castes may exchange services and products with one another, the largest giver is the landed dominant caste or castes who control the most important food, grain.

Do we then, by Marriott's analysis, end up then with a kind of economic model of the caste system? Is purity-impurity an incidental, even epiphenomenal concept? Does a caste's capacity to pollute match the degree of its servitude? This is what Marriott seems to be saying. Yet we still have the problem of why the Potter has a lower-ranking servitude than does the Carpenter, or why the Shoemaker ranks below the Laundryman. To explain such rankings, we must either use the economist's arguments about supply and demand, the sociologist's arguments about difficult-to-acquire skills being more highly valued and ranked, or the Hindu pollution concept which suggests that skills connected with more polluted substances are ranked lower than those connected with less polluted substances. By the Hindu Pollution Concept, the Shoemaker dealing with highly polluted leather, a product of a dead animal, is more polluted than the Washerman who deals with filth of living humans.

How does Marriott reconcile the coded-substance, the *jatidharma* of various transactors, with his emphasis on servitude? Coded-particles are transferred in inter-caste transactions, his ethnosociology says. Marriott, like Dumont and Stevenson, seems left with the problem of the relationship between the coded-particles of jatidharma, so much like purity and pollution, and power relationship of a politico-economic sort epitomized in the dominant caste. Is there any real inconsistency? The serving-and-being-served is the *form* of the relationship. The removal of pollution and avoidance of pollution by the avoidance of certain transactions (the lower caste transmitting polluted food or water to the higher caste) is part of the *content* of such consistently hierarchical relations. That other services may be involved, such as assuring the higher caste patron of various honors, may be accepted as part of the content of the relationship, as well.

The importance of purity relates to the need for the Brahman to be pure in his transactions with the gods. The importance of honor and the submission of the subordinate relates to the need for the king or ruler—in the village, the dominant caste—to carry out his apical role, his kingly style of life.

PURITY-IMPURITY AS SOCIAL INTEGRATOR

The absence during much of Indian history of a single integrated political unit was balanced by the universality of certain cultural institutions. The principle of purity-impurity is especially important in the absence, as well, of an ecclesiastical organization enforcing both hierarchy and caste boundaries.

Despite the lack of an established religious organization, the presence of Brahmans in a region seems to correlate with much more rigorous prohibitions against lower castes. Thus, in South India where Brahmans were not only powerful spiritually but also materially, such prohibitions were very strong. The system is considerably weaker in Ceylon and in the foothills of the Himalayas where there are few Brahmans (Yalman 1967: 61; Srivastava 1966: 188-191; Berreman 1963: 239-240; 1964). Similarly, Untouchability is weaker in the Panjab and in Uttar Pradesh, areas strongly influenced for several hundred years by Muslim rule (Dumont 1970: 58).

Among Christians and Muslims living in India and among Hindus in some overseas communities, caste exists *without* an ideology of purity and pollution—suggesting that this concept is not essential for the existence of caste systems among Indians (Dumont 1970: 46; Pocock 1957; Ahmad 1973). Dumont, who sees the principle of pollution and purity as central in the Hindu caste system, explains these anomalies thus. He hypothesized that the Hindu setting influences Muslim and Christian communities decisively, since each of these non-Hindu religions failed to offer any alternative social structure to displace the already existing pre-conversion caste system (Dumont 1970: 210-211).

Chapter 5

Jati Segments—Again Descent-Groups

JATI SEGMENTS RESIDING WITHIN A VILLAGE

The caste is a large-scale descent-group forming a segment in an interdependent, cooperative, but hierarchical and inegalitarian system. Other castes form the complementary segments of society—each caste specializing in the provision of some commodity or service. The whole system forms a life-scale ritual structure directed toward the double apex of ruler and priest. The dependent and lower-ranking castes provide ruler, priest, and each other with products and services. An especially important service is that of disposing of and absorbing ritual pollution to insure a greater degree of ritual purity for castes of higher rank. It is especially important that priests be ritually pure when they communicate with divine beings whose favor they seek for the welfare of both ruler and society. Their religious services justify the support the priests receive. The ruler or ruling group reciprocates the prestations and support offered by their dependents with the largesse they can provide from their kingdoms or estates (most importantly food grains) and with protection from external attack.

In Chapter 3 the jajmani system in a sample village, Khalapur, was examined. The jati segments to be found within that same village are significant. A jati segment within a village is usually composed of sets of relatives who may be identified as members of one or

86

more lineages. The largest jati, making up over 40
percent of Khalapur's population, was the land-owning
Rajputs. Most Rajput males could trace descent from a
common male ancestor whose sons seem to have settled in
the village in the first half of the sixteenth century
(Hitchcock 1956: 64, 66). Their wives all came from
other villages, since Rajputs, like all other jatis in
Khalapur, rigorously followed the rules of village and
patrilineage exogamy.

The larger jatis in Khalapur are similarly structured, composed of one or more patri-clans. Each patri-
clan is made up of men related to each other by descent
through male links from a common male ancestor. Their
wives, who came from different patri-clans living in
different villages, are also members of the jati, as
are any unmarried children. Sons will marry and remain
in Khalapur. Daughters are supposed to marry into other patri-clans located in other villages. For example,
the Sweepers who lived in the western quarter of Khalapur numbered in 1955 only about 90 persons. The core
of the group was a patrilineage (of 36 persons) tracing
descent from a common ancestor who lived eight generations ago, plus their wives married in from other villages, their unmarried daughters, as well as widows of
men of the lineage and their children. An additional
thirty-six persons were related to this core, either
through daughters of the patriline who had returned after marriage with their children and sometimes with
their husbands to live in their parental village, or
through wives' brothers who had settled with their married sister in her husband's village. This patrilineage plus its accretion of maritally-related families
formed one cognatic descent-group or faction. Another
descent-group composed of the remaining 18 persons was
made up of an elder and the families of his two married
sons plus that of his wife's married sister's family
who had recently migrated to Khalapur from another village.

The membership in factions within a local jati
often coincides with kinship units, as was the case
among the Sweepers (see Lewis 1958: 113-154). Sometimes, however, brothers or patrilineal cousins become
enemies—especially as a result of disputes over the
inheritance of property. Then the male relatives may
align themselves with opposing factions within their

local jati. When a patrilineage is of very large size and great generational depth—in the case of the Rajputs of Khalapur, it was perhaps 500 adult men tracing common descent back 20 generations—the patrilineage itself is typically divided into several factions. Some of these will coincide with a segment of the genealogical tree; some will not, however, and factional composition may be very fluid (see Retzlaff 1962; Hitchcock 1971), or pervasive (Beals and Siegal 1966).

Since members of a jati living in a village are usually relatives by kinship or by marriage, the etiquette of kinship regulates interpersonal relations. Neither Sweepers nor Rajputs spoke of older members of their jati by name alone. Men were "*baba*" (father's father); "*chāchā*" (father's younger brother), "*tao*" (father's older brother); "*phupha*" (father's sister's husband), "*māmā*" (mother's brother), or "*nānā*" (mother's father). Kinship terms were usually extended to members of one's own jati, even if they were unrelated to the speaker. Such terms were even extended to persons of other jatis within the village, especially if the speaker wished to flatter or show affection or good will to the person of another jati.

When any household made an offering to its family gods, the closer relatives were invited to the feast, but a tray of food was always sent to every other house of its lineage or faction. There was at least a taste for every one. And it was customary for all to attend weddings and funerals—coming to the celebrating house to help serve the relatives and guests from other villages and to cooperate in the work to be done.

Jati Councils. Among both the Rajputs and the Sweepers, as well as among the other jatis of Khalapur, the men of a faction had their own *chaupār* (men's sitting platform plus sleeping hall). Here the men and boys gathered in the evenings to discuss present and past events. The sweepers of the western quarter settled most of their family and work problems there, talking things over until the proper course of action seemed to emerge clearly. The older and wiser were listened to most carefully, but every man could speak. Even an impetuous woman, listening from the doorway of her house to the proceedings of the men, might call out some judgment or suggestion.

Jatis of low rank, such as the Sweepers, had a reputation for having effective jati councils (Hutton 1963: 99). Possibly, solidarity is greatest when a group faces considerable oppression, as did the Sweepers at the hands of their Rajput overlords. Many other jatis in Khalapur had effective *panchayats* (councils) — the Shoemakers, the Watercarriers, the Barbers, the Potters, among others.

In the mid-1950s, the Sweepers participated in multi-village Sweeper panchayats composed of representatives of 2, 4, 8, or 12 villages, meeting to take up cases and disputes that a local set of elders had had trouble resolving. Often, panchayats took place when men of several villages came together for a wedding or funeral. Then, after the rites were over, a dispute or case might be aired. The more impartial visitors were likely to see things more clearly than were the local people who might be biased. Thus, a viable solution usually emerged.

Jati panchayats—composed of men of the jati of only one village or a number of villages—settled marital, sexual, and family disputes, and cases of crime and misdemeanors involving members of the jati. The latter included the breaking of jati rules relating to purity and pollution, and to inter-caste relations. The panchayats often functioned as organizations for planning community festivals; for reforming jati customs; for developing community strategy for dealing with the dominant caste; or with the police, or government agents, or the relatives of potential grooms and brides for a local jati's own children, or marital relatives already allied to the jati.

JATIS AS INTERVILLAGE NETWORKS

The word *jati* is used to refer to a caste community within a village, but it is also used to refer to the sets of such village locals or chapters which intermarry. So the Sweepers of Khalapur were related by marriage to Sweepers in many other villages of the area. Since each Sweeper local is likely to be composed of sets of patrilineages plus the adhering marital kin of the patrilineage, the jati then becomes an endogamous group of intermarrying patrilineages. The number of village contingents composing a jati may be many or few. Kathleen Gough reported that the Brahmans of village Kumbapettai, Tanjore District, Tamilnadu, belonged to a set of eighteen intermarrying contingents of Brahmans. Other jatis in Kumbapettai had belonged to units extending over 15 to 31 villages (Gough 1955: 49). Oscar Lewis reported that the Jats of village Rampur, Delhi State, had marital relations with two hundred villages to which they had given daughters in marriage, and with two hundred other villages from which they had taken wives (Lewis 1958: 161). Rather like the Jats of Rampur, the jatis of Khalapur tended to maximize the number of village chapters with which each was allied. None of the jatis in Khalapur gave daughters and took wives from the same set of villages.

Marriage Bonds. Under what circumstances does a jati have "thick" bonds of alliance—that is, many marriages taking place between a pair of village chapters of a jati? Under which circumstances does a jati have "thin bonds"—only one or very few marriages taking place between a pair of villages or lineages?

Marshall Sahlins, writing about tribal societies, has suggested that a prohibition on parallel marriages, the repetition of a marital bond between two localities or lineages, tends to correlate with politically strong lineages. As a result of such a rule, marital ties between localities tend to be weak and thus do not compete with lineal ties (Sahlins 1968: 62-63).

Louis Dumont, on the other hand, has found that some marriages in India are isogamous—that is, the status of the spouses is equal; and some are hypergamous—the wife is of lower status than the husband. Isogamous marriages occur particularly in South India. The connubia there tend to be very small, composed of a few families exactly equal in terms of purity and caste rank; and, more recently, probably equal also in wealth and education. Furthermore, marriage with close relatives such as a mother's brother, or a father's sister's son, or a mother's brother's son is not only allowed, but even preferred. Such marriages can be repeated generation after generation in a kind of perpetual alliance between two lineages, thus forming the "thick" bonds of alliance. In contrast, hypergamous marriages typically take place between ranked lineages, as among such martial castes as the Rajputs in Northern India, and the Marathas in Central India.

Actually, both Sahlins' and Dumont's theories seem to hold true. Both found that "thin" bonds are characteristic of groups with strong patrilineages. Interestingly, the Rajputs and Marathas who have hypergamous marriages are also martial castes with strong political lineages. Dumont suggests that the connubia for castes practicing hypergamy may be very large, since there is not the difficulty of maintaining a group of families of perfect equality (Dumont 1970: 116-117). This latter requirement of the isogamous marriage tends to result in processes of exclusion and fission, as status differences between component families develop. Then families of higher status refuse to marry or eat with those of lower status. Eventually, the absence of association is recognized, and two jatis are perceived where before there was one. Such fission takes place readily in the South Indian isogamous context.

The Individual and His Kindred. The relationship between an individual and his kindred is important in Indian society. A Khalapur villager was likely to have very close relations with his maternal kin—his mother's parents, brothers, the lineage and neighbors residing in his mother's parental village. When a boy ran away from home, the first place to look for him was in his mother's parental village. A Khalapur villager was also likely to have close ties with kin and neighbors of his daughters' husbands, his sisters' husbands, his sons' wives, his brothers' wives, as well as the kin of his own wife. These, the affines, represent a network of persons who would help an individual and whom one was obligated to help.

These relatives from other villages were invited to important family festivities such as weddings, funerals, and birth ceremonies—all of which included formal roles for various relatives. Thus, for example, the mother's father or brother must, by custom, bring gifts when a married daughter or sister had a baby; and a mother's brother must bring a gift when his sister's child weds. In both North India and South India, it is a disgrace if none of the mother's brothers appears to present gifts before his sister's child's wedding. Such presentations are part of the regular wedding schedule of ceremonies. Similarly, the Rajput father's sister has important duties. For example, at a baby's birth in Khalapur, she must wash her brother's wife's breasts before the new mother can nurse the baby. Such institutionalized ceremonial roles keep alive the bonds of the jati inter-village network, as well as immediate kinship ties.

Relations Between the Sexes and Marriage. The preliminaries of marriage arrangements often occur at weddings and funerals. Married daughters who return to enjoy the festivities and to help with the chores and cooking, speak of eligible brides and grooms known to them in their marital villages. Male hosts and guests similarly exchange information. Weddings, funerals, and, to some extent, the less regularly-celebrated birth ceremonies, and celebrations of important Hindu festivals like *Diwāli* or *Holi* bring together relatives and their neighbors from different chapters of a jati located in other villages. Thus, the festivities serve to integrate the jati. Bring together any two strangers of the same jati, and within a short time they will have established connecting links, often calling one another by kin terms and ready to expect hospitality and help from one another.

One of the most rigorous rules for remaining in good standing within any jati is the requirement that one's children marry within that jati. The marriage, of course, will be arranged in keeping with the prohibitions of exogamy mentioned previously. A nightmare for an Indian father would be refusals on the part of all of the appropriate families within his jati to give mates for his children. A family's reputation is, thus, very important. A wayward daughter who runs away with a man of another caste, even if she has been legally wed to that man, must be cut off completely by her parental family. Even with such a severance of ties, it may be difficult for her brothers and sisters to marry properly, within the jati, in the future. A family whose members begin to marry outside of the jati are likely to have to continue to do so, because the more orthodox members of their own jati will refuse to give their children as mates.

Relations between the sexes in India can be understood as molded by the requirements of jati. Thus, for a family to maintain good standing in its jati, it must marry its virginal daughters within the jati to boys not prohibited by rules of intra-caste exogamy.* This is vital for the future marriages of the family's children. Thus, the sexes in Indian societies are usually quite rigorously segregated. Marriages are arranged by elders. Adolescent boys and girls do not talk with one another on social occasions. Even in South India where marriages occur frequently between cross-cousins (a brother's son marrying a sister's daughter, or a brother's daughter marrying a sister's son), the cross-cousins who are of the right relative ages to be potential mates are not allowed to socialize at kin or jati gatherings. Two college-educated South Indian young people agreed that such cross-cousins "might see each other, but would not speak!" Even the more westernized Indians generally do not allow a potential bride and groom to do more than have a brief visit, and that usually in the presence of elders. The arranged marriage, and the prohibition upon socializing with properly related or unrelated members of the opposite sex who are potential marriage partners, are customs related to jati-maintenance. Inter-caste marriage still results in social ostracism of the couple, at least by the kin of the spouse of higher-caste ranking.

For the individual Indian, it is caste in these senses, in terms of his own jati, which is most meaningful to him. The jati members are the people in his neighborhood, usually kinsmen, forming the occupational and status group to which he belongs. They share a common identity both in their own eyes and in the eyes of outsiders. The jati is also the network of relatives and their local groups in other places with whom he and his family maintain contact. Both the localized and the dispersed members of his jati may be considered to form a resource group from whom an individual can seek help and find it (Sharma 1969).

---

*See page 15, *The Gōtra*.

Chapter 6

Social and Cultural Mobility within the Caste System

Most Indians know the names of the larger castes in their region. Although different castes seldom dress distinctively as they once did, Indians can often identify the caste of those they see in public places fairly accurately. So far as other castes go, an Indian is seldom concerned with the identity of the exact jati to which the other belongs; identity of caste is usually sufficient.

IMPORTANCE OF THE VARNA SYSTEM TO CASTE

It is often possible to equate caste in a particular region with the five varnas, and Indians generally do so. As M. N. Srinivas has pointed out, the ancient varnas function as a pan-Indian scheme (Srinivas 1952: 219). They can be considered to form an all-India caste system. In Khalapur, for example, one can identify the Brahmans as Brahmans, the Rajputs as Kshatriyas, the Banias (merchants) as Vaishya, and the Goldsmiths, Carpenters, Blacksmiths, Barbers, Washermen, Watercarriers, Jogis, Mirasis and Gosains as Shudras, and the Shoemakers, the Chamar Leatherworkers, and the Sweepers as Panchalas or Untouchables.

In South India, it is said that there are no Kshatriyas or Vaishya, although some rulers have legitimized themselves as Kshatriyas through Brahmanical

rites of mobility. A large warrior caste, the Nayars
of Kerala, have been considered to be Shudras, not
Kshatriyas; an important caste of traders like the Chet-
tiars are also considered to be Shudras, not Vaishya;
and cultivating landowning caste-clusters like the Vellalas have been considered to be Shudras, not Kshatriyas. Thus, in South India, there are three main blocks
of castes; the Brahmans, the non-Brahmans, and the Untouchables or Adi-Dravidas (original South Indians).

It would appear to be considerably more useful for
an Indian to know the identities of the castes of his
region rather than being concerned with the ancient
varna system. However, the varna system is important
in the process by which a jati or caste attempts to
improve its relative ranking in a local caste hierarchy.
Typically, a Shudra or Untouchable caste argues that
its allocation to a low varna is a mistake, usually an
accident of history whereby the group was cheated out
of its rightful varna status as Brahman or Kshatriya.
Status-legends are claimed to have been discovered
which explain this downward mobility.

During the nineteenth century, when Census-takers
recorded caste membership of residents, claims to high
varna status were often made. Thus, the Shanans of
southern Tamilnadu, whose traditional occupation was
tapping the palmyra tree for its juices used to make
palm sugar and a toddy-drink, claimed that they were
really Kshatriyas, and should be called *Nadars* meaning
"Lord of the Land" (*nad*). They have been successful
insofar as for some decades now they have been known as
Nadars (Hardgrave 1969: 81), although it is doubtful
that non-Nadars consider Nadars to be Kshatriyas.

The Sweepers of Khalapur made two different claims.
One was that they were the descendants of Valmiki, the
author of the Hindu epic, the *Ramayana*; the other was
that they were really Bhil Rajputs, ruling warriors,
who were conquered by Emperor Ashoka (around 250 B.C.)
and then took refuge in the forests. Upon re-entering
village life, they were assigned Untouchable status instead of their proper Kshatriya status (Mahar 1958;
Kolenda 1964). The truth in such a legend would seem
to be something like: we were a tribal people subju-
gated by conquerors of a Hindu kingdom; after conquest,
we continued our tribal life for some time, but then

some of us settled in villages composed of several
Hindu castes; we became such a caste, but one of Untouchable status; we are dissatisfied with that status
and wish to change it.
Such a myth conveys the process of integration of
a tribe into the caste system. The Sweepers of Khalapur had a name, Chuhra, held to be the name of an
earlier Punjabi tribe. Tribals entered the caste system usually in a low-ranking position. In villages of
Bengal today, for example, segments of Santal tribesmen
form jatis of landless agricultural laborers.
There were some tribals who entered Hindu society
with higher varna status. The militarily successful
Gonds of Central India and the Coorgs of Coorgi in
South India successfully claimed Kshatriya varna status.
Some tribal priests, also, succeeded in laying claim to
Brahman varna rank.
The mere assertion of such claims is inadequate if
a jati wishes to succeed in its aspirations to higher
caste rank. In traditional India, one effectively improved rank through force of arms; in modern India,
through wealth; in both traditional and modern India,
through association with those in positions of power.

UPWARD CASTE MOBILITY BEFORE BRITISH RULE

Until the British unification and pacification of the
Indian subcontinent in the first half of the nineteenth
century, the most effective way to rise in the caste
system was by the acquisition of territory either
through conquest, or, if the land had previously been
sparsely populated or empty, by peaceful occupancy.
M. N. Srinivas refers to the former method as "mobility
through resort to warfare." He cites the historian,
K. M. Panikkar, who said that since the fifth century
B.C. "every known royal family has come from a non-
Kshatriya caste" (Srinivas 1955: 8).

Caste and the Conqueror. Since the time of the earliest Indian empire, that of the Mauryans (322 B.C.-183
B.C.), kingdoms, empires, and principalities rose and
fell in various parts of the Indian sub-continent.
While many of these areas were ruled by Muslims, or by

Christians after European conquests, those ruled by
Hindus were often controlled by members of jatis of
lowly varna. Thus, a peasant jati that owned much land
might translate its grain tribute into payment for
troops and weapons, and might capture more territory
and establish a kingdom. In the ancient varna system,
rulers should be Kshatriyas; often such peasant conquerors made claims to being Kshatriyas. The jati and
the caste of such conquerors, partly through the ruler's dependence upon his kinsmen for support, likewise
rose to Kshatriya rank.

Shivaji, the great Maratha conqueror of central
India in the eighteenth century, may serve as an example. The Moghul empire, which had dominated much of
India in the seventeenth century, was in decline by the
early eighteenth century. Shivaji's father had been a
jagirdar or vassal to the Muslim ruler of Bijapur, a
principality subordinate to the Moghul emperor. Shivaji overthrew the Moghul rule and established his own
Hindu empire from the Arabian Sea to the Bay of Bengal.
His caste, the Maratha, was considered to be of Shudra
varna, so Shivaji went through a religious rite of
transition into Kshatriyahood. Along with Shivaji's
rise in varna status, his caste, the Marathas, also
came to have Kshatriya rank (Srinivas 1968: 189; Marriott 1968 a: 112-113).

Caste Rise by Serving Rulers. Jatis whose members
served either Hindu or non-Hindu rulers likewise at-
tained higher varna rank. For example, the Patidars of
Gujarat, another peasant group of Shudra varna, supported the Maratha descendents of Shivaji, the Gaekwads,
who ruled Central Gujarat. Gradually, claiming to be
Kshatriyas, they established their own small regimes
(Shah 1964). Another example of a rise in caste
through service to rulers is the Kayasthas, a caste of
scribes. The Kayasthas made themselves useful first to
the Moghuls, then to the British rulers. While they
were a low caste in the twelfth century, by the nineteenth century the Kayasthas in Northern India had
risen to the "twice-born" category, although jatis in
the Kayastha caste further to the east in Bengal remained Shudras (Cohn in Silverberg 1968: 122-123).
Similarly, Brahman *purohits* (family chaplains),

attached to the Khatris of the Punjab, benefited from
the Khatris' patronage. As recipients of such benefits,
the Brahmans were not unsympathetic to claims by Shudra
castes, such as the Khatris, to Kshatriya status (Rowe
1968 b: 203).

Burton Stein, an historian, finds that in medieval
South India, families rose through association with
Muslim rulers. The unit of mobility was not the jati
or caste, but the family or a group of families (Stein
1968). Srinivas suggests that such familial upward
mobility was likely to result in the formation of a new
jati out of an established larger one. A few families
which intermarried closely could become a closed endogamous jati, claiming a separate identity and higher
rank than the jati of origin. This was possible especially in South India where near relatives such as
cross-cousins or uncle and niece were preferred marriage partners. By such close marriages, a jati of a
few families could be established relatively easily in
two generations (Srinivas 1968: 196).

An orthodox Hindu ruler considered it his duty to
uphold the caste system within his kingdom. He had
authority over caste matters including the right to
outcast, the raising and lowering of jati ranks enforcing Untouchability, and issuing marriage regula-
tions (Smith 1963: 298-299). Such power continued
into the twentieth century in non-British India, the
one-third of the sub-continent composed of princely
states, most of them ruled by Hindus. Such powers in
the hands of the ruler probably continue today in
Nepal, still an independent Hindu kingdom.

UPWARD CASTE MOBILITY UNDER BRITISH RULE

The British assumed similar control when recording jati
identities in Census enumerations. From 1891 to 1931,
the Censuses report numerous efforts on the part of
middle and low castes to have themselves registered as
members of twice-born varnas. These claims reached a
peak when Herbert Risley, the Census Commissioner for
the 1901 Census, tried to rank all castes. Hundreds of
jatis tried to ensure a higher rank by claiming high
varna titles. For example, the Kurmi cultivators of

Bengal wanted to be Kurmi Kshatriyas; the Teli Oil-pressers wanted to be called Vaishyas. Evidence from myths and so-called history was offered for each claim. Inter-jati rivalries were common, as some jatis tried to divorce their identity from that of jatis of their own caste which they considered to be inferior. Castes already established as Kshatriyas or Brahmans or Vaishya also complained about the interlopers to *their varna* (Rowe 1968a: 66-68; 1968b: 203; Srinivas 1968: 195).

One Census official for Bengal received enough petitions to weigh 120 pounds from jatis which wanted to have varna titles or wanted to take the name of a higher-ranking jati. Finally, district committees were set up to evaluate these claims, most of which were not sustained. Of course, one official district committee might approve high varna for a segment of a caste in its district, while the same petition might be rejected for another segment of the same caste in another district. A ruling in a jati's favor was looked upon as positive proof of the jati's claims. By such rulings, the British government functioned in somewhat the same way as the Hindu kings had in adjudicating caste affairs. (Since 1931, the Censuses of India have ceased recording jati identities.)

SANSKRITIZATION

Claims to "twice-born" varna status, along with the justifications for such claims, were made in the process of what M. N. Srinivas has called "Sanskritization." Nowadays, in the secular Indian state, there is no official arbiter for claims to higher rank. However, jatis continue to try to improve their rank in local caste hierarchies by changing the general public's view of their jati's rank, a kind of arbitration by public opinion.

Sanskritization refers to the efforts made by lower castes to emulate the Brahman style of life. If possible, a jati adopts Sanskrit ritual and hires the services of Brahman priests. In the attempts to be granted higher caste rank through purifying their customs, a jati may give up a defiling occupation. Thus, Chamar leather workers in northern India have very largely given up working on leather or retrieving dead animals for jajmans, and Balais in Rajasthan have given up making shoes. A jati may adopt vegetarianism; or, at any rate, a less defiling diet. For example, the Khatiks near Benares have given up keeping pigs. A jati may also give up drinking liquor, or it may prohibit widow-remarriages as gestures of purification.

In his later work, Srinivas broadened his concept of Sanskritization to include emulation of dominant castes of any high varna. Lynch has called this "elite emulation" (Lynch 1969: 218). Beck found that the set of castes called "right-hand" castes in the Kongu area of Tamilnadu emulated the dominating cultivator caste, while "left-hand" castes there emulated Brahmans (Beck 1972). Barnett has spoken of the kingly model (as distinct from the Brahman model). Both Brahman and Kshatriya or kingly models serve as referents for castes in another part of Tamilnadu (Barnett 1970).

Supplementing such elite emulation, an upwardly mobile jati may try to improve its status by "pulling rank"—refusing to take food or water from the jati of next highest rank. Thus, the Sweepers of Khalapur were trying to prohibit their members from taking food at weddings of the Leatherworkers, the caste next highest to them in rank in Khalapur. Some of the Sweepers' leaders also talked about refusing to serve Laundrymen, who were of even higher rank and in the Shudra category, as a challenge to the relative rank ordering of the Sweepers and Laundrymen.

M. N. Srinivas has claimed that Untouchables are never able to cross the line into Shudra rank (Srinivas 1962: 58). There are some instances where this has occurred. Laundrymen in Western Uttar Pradesh are considered to be Shudras; in Eastern Uttar Pradesh, they are considered to be Untouchables.

Sanskritization is probably at best a very slow method for a jati to raise its status. It is likely to be successful only if reinforced by economic or political power. An instance of success through economic power is that of the Noniyas of Eastern Uttar Pradesh in Northern India. Traditionally, the Noniyas' work was making salt and moving earth. During the second

half of the nineteenth century and up to the time of
the First World War, however, some of them made money
as contractors on government roads, bridges, and public
works. One of them founded the Rajput Advancement Society to encourage Noniyas to claim to be Chauhan Rajputs. The organization and its idea spread gradually
throughout the areas where Noniyas lived. It involved
initiation with the sacred thread, and the writing of a
body of literature supporting their claim to having
been the Rajputs defeated at Delhi with King Prithvi
Raj in the twelfth century. They claimed to have then
been scattered—some moving into eastern Uttar Pradesh.
In the village of Senapur, where William Rowe studied
a local contingent of Noniyas, he found that they had
considerably improved their local caste ranking over
half a century. From holding a rank bordering upon the
Untouchable category they had risen in the village
caste hierarchy to a rank of tenth or eleventh—a position firmly in the upper part of the Shudra category.
In the mid-1950s they were being served by Brahman
priests; their goddess was now vegetarian, no longer
taking "blood" (animal) sacrifices, and they kept their
brides in *parda* (seclusion), all indications of Sanskritization. They even wore the sacred thread, although their doing so was at first violently opposed by
the Thakur dominant caste of Senapur who considered
themselves to be the Kshatriyas and considered the
Noniyas to be Shudras. So in the Noniyas' case their
efforts to attain higher caste rank succeeded after
their economic status had greatly improved.

David Pocock has described the advancement in
caste rank of traditional peasant cultivators, the *Kan-
bis* of Gujerat, due to British favor. In 1931, they
officially changed their caste name to the more honor-
ific *Patidārs*, and today they are considered to be of
equal rank with the Vaishyas (Pocock 1955).

A frequent result of efforts to Sanskritize customs was division of a jati into two parts—the segment which had successfully Sanskritized some of its
customs, and the segment which had not. The former
segment would "pull rank" on the latter by refusing
to give daughters in marriage to its members, they
might or might not receive brides from the less Sanskritized segment. Thus the effect of elite emulation
was to proliferate the number of existing jatis.

The proliferation of jati units due to divisions resulting from Sanskritization and elite emulation may be a feature of stability in the Indian caste system. Thus, Hindu society is not composed of a small aristocracy and a large mass. If the twice-born is equivalent to an "aristocracy," within that aristocracy there are many rankings. Likewise, among the Shudras and Untouchables, there are rankings, based largely on customs relating to the purity-pollution values. Such distinctions in purity rankings prevented the development of feelings of unity among the Indian "masses," or for that matter, among the "aristocracy." Since interaction between persons of different jati almost always involved a purer person interacting with a less pure person, any joint effort implied one individual's being polluted by the other. Since pollution was undesirable, if for no other reason than the danger of being an outcasted from one's own jati, joint efforts by jatis of different rank were prevented. Competition for rank in terms of the purity-pollution values effectively fragmented society, so that substantial numbers of lower castemen were unlikely to join together to change the caste system itself or to overthrow those in control. In modern contexts to which pollution concepts are not applied, fusion of castes contiguous in rank is more likely to occur.

THE EFFECT OF EDUCATION ON CASTE

In understanding Sanskritization, one must recognize that access to modern education on the part of some of a caste's members is usually one of the preconditions. Especially important for Shudras and Untouchables were schools established during the nineteenth and twentieth century. In response to Christian proselytizing, reform movements within Hinduism, such as the Arya Samaj and Brahmo Samaj, were established. These movements included in their programs the establishment of schools at which lower-caste pupils were sometimes accepted. The Jatavs, studied by Lynch, developed some educated members by sending their sons to Christian mission, Arya Samaj, and government schools (Lynch 1969:68-69).

William Rowe found in his study of Noniyas that younger educated men had little interest in Sanskritization of their caste customs, but great interest in political channels to power (Rowe 1968: 75). Similarly, Owen Lynch found that the efforts of upward mobility on the part of the Jatav Untouchable Shoemakers of Agra City changed over the course of the twentieth century from Sanskritization, including claims to Kshatriya varna rank, to conversion to Buddhism, and participation in the Republican Party. Influenced early in the twentieth century by a Hindu reform movement known as the Arya Samaj, the Jatavs made claims to being of Kshatriya varna. They sent some of their young men to school, and they organized to Sanskritize the caste. During the 1930s, when the Independence movement was strong, the Jatavs followed the lead of the Untouchable national leader, Ambedkar, and identified themselves as a Scheduled Caste. Then, in the 1950s, they converted to Buddhism. In 1958, many formed the Republican Party of Agra, the political expression of the "new Buddhists" who were working for political power for Untouchables. Thus, the Jatavs moved from Sanskritization, with its explicit support of the caste system (even though such efforts challenge the dominant caste and the established caste order), to politicization with explicit attack upon the caste system in a new democratic order (Lynch 1969). In Chapter 10 more will be said about this latter process.

WEALTH AND CASTE

Attainment of wealth, especially in the form of land, may enable a jati to sustain a luxurious style of life with much leisure time for its members and servants to carry on the menial work on the land. Such a process seems to account for the gradual and undramatic transformation of the identities of some lower peasant jatis into those of higher rank. Ghurye has mentioned the numerous Kunbis in Maharashtra who have transformed themselves into the higher-ranking Marathas (Ghurye 1960: 110). Kathleen Gough speaks of cultivating castes who, either through raiding or through mercenary soldiering for rajas, gained control over lands

in Tanjore, in Tamilnadu. These castes then Sanskritized their customs and began calling themselves by the
more aristocratic title, *Vellāla*. Gough quotes a local
saying, "Kallans, Maravans, and Agamudaiyans, becoming
fat, turn into Vellalas" (Gough 1960: 57).

RANK WITHIN A CASTE

There are a number of castes which include within them
subgroups of varying status and occupation and, possibly, of differing ethnic origin. Henry Orenstein refers to such castes as "loosely structured" and gives
as examples the Kolis and Marathas of Maharashtra.
Thus, Marathas seem to include all high clean Hindu
castes except the vegetarian castes of Brahmans, Gurava
(temple priests), and Sonars (Goldsmiths). Kolis include a variety of Shudra castes ranking below Marathas
and above Untouchables (Orenstein 1963, 1965). Marathas did not have ranked subcastes; instead, they had
"roughly ranked bilateral kindred" with some sets of
households looking upon others as lower or higher (Orenstein 1965: 125). Subgroupings varying in rank occur
also among the Nayar of Kerala. There were royal lineages, lineages of district chiefs, lineages of village
headmen, and several sub-castes of commoners (Gough
1959). Similar differences in rank with some aristocratic and some commoner lineages within one caste occur among Kallas of Tanjore (Gough 1960).
    Thus, hierarchy may occur both between castes and
within castes. Such diversity within a caste probably
comes about as some lineages have made successful conquests to become royal lines or as some lower castes
have successfully laid claim to a new caste title and
been integrated as a lower sub-caste. Such diversity
in occupation and rank has occurred more recently by
means of education and the taking up of businesses and
professions by educated caste members. An excellent
work showing this process of caste differentiation is
Robert Hardgrave's study of the Nadars, traditional
toddy-tappers of Tamilnadu (Hardgrave 1969).
    There have, in fact, been cases when a jati seg-
ment has moved to a new place and claimed to be of a
caste of higher rank. Adrian Mayer has observed some

attempts at "passing" as a higher caste and finds that
the process of acceptance of such jatis is slow, because the natives of the new place cannot ascertain the
correctness of the claims (Mayer 1960: 27-28). Thus,
in the case of one jati claiming to be Brahmans, villagers would not take food from them, because there was
doubt about the genuineness of their claimed identity.

DOWNWARD MOBILITY

There are various processes of downward mobility in the
caste system. Some have already been implied. When a
ruling group was conquered, it lost rank. Another process of downward mobility involves outcasting. Louis
Dumont found that there was a segment of Pramalai Kallar (a dominant caste in parts of Madurai district,
Tamilnadu Shudras, formerly known for their raiding and
thievery) with whom the rest of the Pramalai Kallar
would not marry. The group seemed to have been descendants of "irregular unions," presumably marriages between a Kallar and a mate of lower caste (Dumont 1957:
149-150). Since intermarriage between persons of different varna is the explanation which Hindu books of
religious law give for the proliferation of castes,
such evidence as the impure group of Pramalai Kallar
can be viewed as support for the classical theory (Dumont 1957: 12).
     What about individuals? Do individuals sometimes
try to pass themselves off as members of different jati
other than their own? It is difficult for an individual to survive in India without relatives. Even in
migrating from village to city, it would be unusual for
an individual to go alone (Rowe 1973). Harold Isaacs
suggests that educated Untouchables, by being well-
spoken and well-dressed, often appear to be members of
higher caste (Isaacs 1965: 143-149). Or they may even
claim to be of a different caste for temporary benefits.
However, the need for mates for one's children, and
relatives for ceremonial participation and as a resource group in other ways, discourages permanent passing.
     The dissatisfied male member of all jatis always
has had the possibility of dropping out of the caste

system entirely by becoming a holy man. In so doing, he severs his membership in family, village, and caste. Dumont sees this as the individualistic balance to the essentially collectivistic caste system. Renunciation is an escape-hatch in the caste system (Dumont 1970). While there are holy women, they are very few in number, and almost all are older, beyond their childbearing years.

Chapter 7

Revolts against the Caste System?

In the preceding chapter, fragmentation in social structure was seen to be a consequence of commitment to the Hindu purity complex as a basis for ranking castes. The likelihood of large blocks of castes coalescing into contending units has occurred only recently. Why, in the past, were there no revolts against the caste system? Why did Untouchables and lower castes endure their disprivilege?

LOCAL REVOLTS

To answer these questions, a distinction must be made between massive revolts engaging peasants of an entire region, and petty local revolts. With respect to small local revolts, the answers seem to come down to these three:

First, if a discontented caste had military might, it could conquer a dominant caste in a locality and become the dominant caste itself. In general, historians have not viewed such dissension for decisive power as movement *against* the caste system, but as the normal political struggle between petty chiefs. In this book, such movements are seen as processes of social mobility *within* the caste system, not as movements against the caste system.

Second, a discontented contingent of a servant or artisan jati could leave its locality of residence. In

107

fact, there is probably a great deal of flux in the
membership of local jati communities—both individuals
and families continually moving into other villages.
Some of this flux is culturally-given; married women
often live part of the time in their husband's village
and part of the time in their father's village. Yet
there is undoubtedly a strong alternative residence
pattern to the usual Indian rule of patrilocality, such
as families residing in the mother's father's village,
or the father's sister's husband's village. An entire
jati contingent might leave one village to work for a
dominant caste in another village. Until recent decades, the main problem for the landed was to retain
agrestic servants. The servants' bargaining power was
undoubtedly greater in the past than it is at the
present time. Similarly, jajmani servants, especially
those making a product in demand, could relocate fairly
easily. Even now, many Carpenters and Washermen can
move readily to other villages needing their skills and
services.

Third, during past centuries, the weak needed to
be protected by those with force of arms, whether a
local dominant caste, a local nobleman, or raja. As
mentioned before, the lower castes exchanged services
and products for protection by the dominant powers.

The above reasons why violent revolt did not occur
all support the claim that there was room for maneuver
for the individual and jati contingent *within* the caste
system. With the exception of some slaves, lower
castes did have some bargaining power either to better
their position in a locality or to move to a new locality. However, there is no question that members of
dominant castes were sensitive to infringement on high-
caste prerogatives. Thus, lower-castemen who adopted
the sacred thread or who tried to give up defiling
services performed for higher caste jajmans were punished. This kind of interaction was discussed in Chapter 5 on caste mobility and appears again in the dis-
cussion of reform movements among Untouchables in
Chapter 8.

LARGE-SCALE REVOLT

As for large-scale massive revolts, few have occurred
in India. Barrington Moore, Jr. has pointed out that
although Indian peasants have been as economically-
deprived as those in China, massive peasant revolts
have seldom occurred in India, whereas they occurred
often in pre-modern China (Moore 1966: 315, 379). Although peasant revolts have been relatively few and of
limited geographical scope in India, a number of scholars (Chaudhuri 1955, 1957; Natarajan 1953; Fuchs 1965;
Moore 1966; Gough 1974) have reviewed some of those
which have occurred. The most recent review by Gough
is an analysis of seventy-seven peasant uprisings during late Moghul, British, and contemporary Indian rule
(Gough 1974). Gough finds that caste has not operated
as a barrier to the organization of large numbers of
peasants during severe economic deprivation—provided
that effective leaders emerged. In fact, in some instances the inter-village jati network provided a system of communication during uprisings. None of these
uprisings were directed against the caste system; and
in most cases the participants were tribal peoples,
rather than caste-ordered peasant villagers. One of
the few revolts involving peasants, rather than tribals, was the Deccan riots of 1875. These were directed against moneylenders; the aim of the revolt was
to destroy records of the onerous mortgages and debts
burdening the people. During the British period, land
became a saleable commodity, and moneylenders amassed
land by foreclosing mortgages, thus impoverishing the
previous cultivating owners (Catanach 1966). The riots
were the peasants' reaction to the consequences of the
new status of land.

COMMUNIST-LED UPRISINGS

Since the independence of India in 1947, there have
been five communist-led uprisings:

  1. In Tebhaga, Northern Bengal, in 1946, when
      sharecroppers demanded higher shares.

2. In Telangana, Andhra Pradesh, between 1946 and 1948, when peasants demanded the abolition of illegal exactions by landlords, and the cancellation of debts.

3. In Tanjore, Tamilnadu, in 1948, demanding rent-reduction and the doubling of wages for landless laborers.

4. In Naxalbari, West Bengal, in 1967, during which tribal peasant unions redistributed land.*

5. In Andhra Pradesh in 1969 when a movement similar to that in Naxalbari took place in some districts.

In the last two uprisings, rebel unions held sizeable amounts of territory for considerable periods of time, and numbers of landlords, police, moneylenders, and bureaucrats were executed before the unionists were defeated (Gough 1974: 1403-1404).

The evidence on agrarian uprisings does not suggest militance against the caste system *per se*. Undoubtedly the dominant castes, persons, or families in the areas involved were affected, although careful studies of the interface between local caste systems and the classification of social segments *vis-à-vis* land have not yet been published. The disemployment of large numbers of landless and land-poor rural people, most of whom are Untouchables or of low-caste rank, makes available an army for a peasant revolution.

In his careful study of modern peasant revolutions, Joel Migdal finds that severe deprivation in itself does not stimulate peasants to revolt. Peasants participating in revolution are those who are already engaged in marketing cash crops and who find themselves in an abruptly unstable market situation. Thus, it is the economically better-off or "middle peasants" who organize for revolt or reform first. Migdal's review of peasant participation in the Chinese Communist revolution shows that organization is a long, slow process, carried out by an educated leadership of students, intellectuals, and alienated members of the middle-class (Migdal 1974: 229-237).

---

*Non-tribal peasants were not involved.

POLITICAL PARTIES AND CASTE

Are the land-poor and landless, who are increasing both in number and in their proportion of the rural Indian population, Communist? Studies by political scientists indicate that the allegiances of lower castes and Untouchables are as widely distributed among the array of political parties as are the allegiances of middle or higher castes. Also, the leadership in the Communist and Socialist political parties in India, like the leadership of the more central Congress and rightist parties, are men of high-caste status. Only the SSP, a socialist party in Bihar, and one of the Communist parties in Kerala have had moderate success in integrating men of low-caste status into leadership positions (Brass 1973: 14-15; 109). Of course as we shall see in Chapter 10, some sections of Untouchables, most particularly the Mahars of Maharashtra, have formed political parties of their own.

In summary, the caste system of the past which was a patronage system integrating poor and rich, is gradually dying out; and there appears to be no new system, not even a revolutionary movement, ready to absorb the casualties resulting from the transformation of the Indian rural social structure.

Chapter 8

Hinduism and the Caste System

Hinduism is a complex collection of philosophies and religious beliefs and practices. All are directed toward winning salvation, or freedom from rebirth; but only some support directly the caste system. The various approaches to salvation are called *margs*. There is, for example, the *dharma marg*, the path of duty which most clearly supports the caste system; the *karma marg*, the path of ritual activity, which supports the caste system because of the great ritual importance of the Brahman; the *jnana marg*, the path of mysticism; and the *bhakti marg*, the path of salvation through belief and devotion to a personal savior. The jnana and and bhakti margs do not support the caste system directly. However, in their preoccupation with divine powers, they do not advocate concern with or attack upon the caste social order.

DHARMA MARG—FULFILLMENT OF DUTY

In Chapter 3, Marriott's and Inden's theory of the vital importance of dharma as the code in the coded-substance which makes the Hindu person's body was shown.

The concept of dharma marg or the path to salvation through fulfillment of duty, including caste duty, staunchly supports the caste system. The *Bhagavad Gita*, probably the best known Hindu religious work, teaches that it is better to do one's own caste duty badly rather than the duty of another caste well.

Vangala J. Ram, in a recent analysis of the themes in North Indian village culture, emphasizes the importance of dharma or duty. He says:

> This theme of dharma runs so deep into Indian culture that many regard it as synonymous with it. Almost every form of social action is attributable to this overriding concept. . . . A fieldworker in an Indian village, very early in his field work, is confronted with dharma as the explanation of actions for which the informant can offer no other explanation. But when he stops to ask what this dharma is, he comes across only vague and nebulous responses. Dharma is a strong motivating force which even those who are impelled by it are unable to explain. To violate one's *dharma* is unthinkable. The charge of "*adharma*" (contravention of *dharma*) is one of the most serious charges that can be leveled against anyone.
>
> All behavior is viewed in the context of duty or *dharma*. The Brahman avoids contact with Camars, devotes himself to learning, and accepts gifts, because it is his *dharma* to do so; a Camar serves his Thakur, often at his own expense, because that is *his dharma*; . . . a Camar defers to his Thakur, stands up when the latter passes, lets him initiate a conversation, and addresses him respectfully, because that is what he has been told is his *dharma*. However much it might displease him . . . he will continue to do it, because *dharma* cannot be violated. One's opinions, attitudes and feelings cannot stand up against the overwhelming power of *dharma*.
>
> (Ram 1971: 315)

The prominent Indologist, Heinrich Zimmer, recounts this story as an illustration of the ancient Hindu belief that perfect performance of dharma not only leads to salvation but to immense personal power. The story is this:

> The great emperor Ashoka was standing by the river Ganges with his ministers and people, near

his capital city of Pataliputra (nowadays, Patna, Bihar). He asked if any of his very gifted colleagues could make the river run backwards, in the opposite direction. None could, but there was standing within earshot a courtesan, Bindumati, who performed the feat—the river reversed its flow. The emperor in amazement asked the courtesan how it was she had performed this "act of truth." She explained that she had always fulfilled her dharma consistently, unquestioningly. She served whomever gave her money, she said, whether he be a Kshatriya, a Brahman, a Vaishya, or a Shudra. She treated all her customers exactly alike, did her duty, and thus through her perfect dharma had great magical power.

(Zimmer 1951: 161-162)

Brahmanism. Orthodox Brahmanism states that only Brahmans can gain salvation; those of other castes must wait until they are reborn as Brahmans and then perhaps they will be able to transcend the rebirth process by becoming part of the Absolute. The path of works, the karma marg, which includes the performance by Brahmans of the prescribed religious sacrifices, is the most orthodox path. Higher caste families are regular clients of household preceptors who perform the various annual Hindu rites for them. The very important Hindu Pollution Concept which is so basic to the ranking of castes in local caste systems is connected with the predominance of the Brahman priest. He must be kept pure, so there must be others in other castes to absorb impurity for him (and, as it turns out, for other high varnas or castes as well).

OTHER PATHS

Buddhism, Jainism, and the Upanishads. As early as 500 B.C. there were teachers who rejected the Brahman priests' claim of superiority and the exclusive truth of the Brahmans' ritual tradition, the Vedas. One of these teachers was Buddha; another was Mahavira, the founder of Jainism. The teachings of both were considered by Brahmans to be heresies and, thus, outside

of Brahmanism. Within the Vedic tradition, however,
were the *Upanishads*, the insights of mystics. All
three of these teachings, Buddhism, Jainism, and the
Upanishads, developed during the same period, and all
discounted the Brahman sacrifices as the most important
path to salvation. All three held as the ideal a totally religious individual, a mystic Holy Man. Within
Hinduism the path to salvation through such mysticism
is the jnana marg.

The Holy Man as Renouncer of Caste. The individual who
renounces village, caste, and family to become a holy
man has been released as an individual from the caste
system. Louis Dumont has spoken of the ideal of the
Renouncer as the individualistic alternative to the
collectivistic caste system within Hindu culture. Dumont points out that it is the Renouncers as religious
philosophers who have been the creative force within
Hinduism; not the orthodox priestly Brahmans (Dumont
1970a: 46). Renouncers as "holy-men" are not totally
divorced from society. They both teach ordinary men
and depend upon ordinary men for food and shelter as
they tour the countryside. The various *bhakti* or devotional approaches taught by *gurus* or "holy-men" held
that through love and devotion to a savior one could
reach salvation. These holy men rejected the necessity
of the Brahman intermediary, as well as the caste ladder of ascent to rebirth. The hymns and poems of the
bhakti cults were written by saints of a variety of
caste origins. One of the most popular was a Weaver
named Kabir; another was a Shoemaker named Raidas.
There were women poets, also, such as Mira Bai. Thus,
much of the inspirational leadership was held by non-
Brahmans, who were often of humble caste rank. In
this sense, the bhakti sects were anti-Brahman—
rejecting the priest as intermediary, and holding out
hope for direct salvation.

Bhakti Marg and Caste. *Bhajan* groups which gather for
hymn singing in a bhakti mode are often multi-caste in
membership. There were such group in Khalapur. Milton
Singer also describes these multi-caste groups in the
city of Madras (Singer 1972: 199-241). However, the
bhakti spirit of intercaste communal devotion does not

seem to have affected the local functioning ritual-
occupational caste systems; they remain intact. The
content of the bhakti beliefs concerns the perfection
of the savior and his or her powers of salvation.
There is little direct criticism of the social order.
In fact, people converting to bhakti sects in past centuries have formed new castes (Dumont 1970: 188), so
that sectarian castes constitute a minor number of
castes in the local caste systems. In Khalapur, for
example, there were both Weavers and Kabir Panthi
Weavers, the latter following the bhakti guru, Kabir.
In the state of Karnataka (formerly Mysore) one of the
major dominant castes is such a bhakti sect, the $Vira$-
$\acute{s}aivas$, popularly known by the phallic pendant ($lingam$,
symbol of the god $\acute{S}iva$) which they wear as Lingayats.

Dumont suggests that the religious support for
the caste system lies in the purity-impurity syndrome
which, in turn, implies the necessity of the Brahman
priest and other twice-born men to be in a pure state
for Vedic study and ritual communication with the gods.
Thus, caste is closely related to karma marg (the path
of ritual action). To the extent that bhakti and jnana
paths reject these assumptions, such disciplines do not
support the caste system as a religious system. However, they allow it to continue as a secular order of
society. Dumont points out that this religio-social
phenomenon, the relationship of these individualistic
paths to the caste system, is poorly understood by
scholars (Dumont 1970: 186-187).

OTHER RELIGIONS AND CASTE

Other religions have also seemingly offered an alternative to Hinduism and, one might suppose, to the caste
system. Thus, during the Muslim rule of large parts
of India from the eleventh to the twentieth century,
many Hindus converted to Islam, a religion which holds
that all are equal in the eyes of Allah. Today, about
10 percent of the population of India is Muslim. Before the partition of the subcontinent into India and
the Muslim nation of Pakistan, about one-quarter of the
population was Muslim.

The inspiration of Islam is seen in some of the medieval Bhakti cults and in the reform religion, *Sikhism*, which developed in the fifteenth century in Northwest India, Sikhism was anti-Brahman, anti-caste, and anti-idolatry. In some parts of India, Christian missionaries were quite successful. In areas such as Kerala and Southern Tamilnadu, where there were many Untouchables and low castes, and where the rules of pollution were strong, large numbers converted to Christianity. Pressentday Kerala has a relatively high proportion of Christians, about 20 percent (Nayar 1966: 176).

Such religious counter-movements to caste were unsuccessful in that Christians, Muslims, and Sikhs were integrated as castes into the caste system. Among Christians, Sikhs, and Muslims, there are also castes—their ranking and separation based upon the Hindu origin of the converts. Thus, *Mazhbis* were Untouchables converted to Sikhism. There are in Tamilnadu, Nadar Christians and Pariah (Untouchable) Christians, and they do not worship together.

REFORM MOVEMENTS WITHIN HINDUISM

Growing out of the contact with Christian beliefs, various reform movements within Hinduism developed during the nineteenth century. Among the most important are the *Brahmo Samaj*, *Arya Samaj*, and *Ramakrishna Mission*. All were somewhat critical of the caste system, but their influences in this respect touched mostly urban, western-educated men.

In conclusion, there were religious approaches both within Hinduism and in other popular religions that failed to support the religious importance of the Brahman and the ladder to salvation through rebirth into higher and higher castes. However, this lack of support had little effect upon the caste system as a lived in social order because none of the other religions offered or instituted a new alternative social order. All were, in this sense, "other-worldly."

Chapter 9

Caste and Politics

INDIA UNDER BRITISH RULE

In the first half of the nineteenth century, not only did the British conquerors encourage Christian missionaries, but reform-minded governor-generals instituted laws against such extreme Hindu practices as *sati* (the burning of a widow on her husband's funeral pyre), infanticide, and human sacrifice. Percival Spear, a noted historian, believes that "fear of the loss of caste," a belief that the British rulers "meant to destroy their caste" explains, in part, the Mutiny of 1857 when the Indian *Sipahis* (enlisted men) of the Army of Bengal rebelled against their British officers. Spear explains that liberal governor-generals and other officials hoped to acculturate Indians to Western values. The decision was taken to educate an elite through English medium instruction; this was seen by some Indians as a threat to Sanskritic and Arabic instruction. Railroad carriages, in which the ritual rules relating to caste separation were not enforced, began to ply the country. Considerable numbers of Brahman caste members from Oudh were in the Bengal Army. They were resentful because their princely state, Oudh, was integrated into British India in 1856. Then, there was an enlistment act which required new recruits to agree to serve overseas—a violation of a Hindu prohibition on overseas travel. Also, the introduction of gun cartridges, said to be greased with animal fat, that the sepoy had to bite to use was offensive to both Hindus and Muslims in the army (Spear 1961: 270-271). An outcome of the 1857 Mutiny was a British decision to respect traditional Indian customs and to desist from reform (*Ibid.*, 279-280). However, the necessity of knowing English in order to work in a British company or in the British-run government of India had been well-learned before the Mutiny. Many educated Indians were frustrated by British policies preventing Indians from occupying high positions in government. They resorted to political activity to change British government policies. By the early twentieth century, Indians were demanding the independence of India from Britain. The Indian leaders, men like Jawarharlal Nehru and Mahatma Gandhi, were all English-educated; their thinking was dominated by English political ideals. In the 1940s they led a movement to establish parliamentary democracy in a secular Indian state with universal suffrage and equality of all before the law. These were not traditional Hindu ideas; they were Western in origin.

ANTI-BRAHMAN POLITICAL MOVEMENTS

For over one hundred years, there were specifically anti-Brahman political movements, the earliest in Maharashtra in the mid-nineteenth century. In recent decades, such movements have been strongest in the South Indian states of Tamilnadu, Karnataka, and Kerala, where laws relating to government service and places in government-run universities have been written to pointedly discriminate *against* Brahmans.

These laws are a reaction to the dominance up to about 1920 of Brahmans in government service, and to the disproportionate number of Brahmans among students in institutions of higher education. The traditional role of Brahmans as *literati* and counselors of kings throughout Indian history perhaps explains the Brahmans' ready efforts in the nineteenth century to learn English and to get government jobs in British-ruled India. In South India Brahmans had also been large landowners, and thus had had secular as well as religious power.

The Dravidian Movement. Early in the twentieth century, there developed in South India a strong Dravidian
movement. (*TiraviDam*, or *Dravidam*, is "the Tamil country; the Tamil language; or the country South of the
Vindya mountains," according to Lifeco's Tamil dictionary.) The Dravidian chauvinists argue that there was a
casteless Tamil culture in South India before the Aryan
culture arrived in the centuries just before the Christian era. According to the movement's interpretation
of history, the Dravidians then allowed themselves to
be dominated by the Brahmans and their teachings. During the 1950s and 1960s, the Dravidian chauvinists
adopted an anti-Aryan attitude toward North India.
They saw the national Congress Party, which organized
the national government, as a body of North Indians
oppressing South Indians.

Early anti-Brahman parties included the Justice
Party founded in 1916, the Self-Respect Movement
founded in 1925, and the *Dravida Kazagham* (Dravidian
Federation) founded in 1944. The D.K. demanded a separate Dravidian State which would be casteless and
egalitarian. According to the D.K. adherents, it had
been North Indian Brahmans who introduced the caste
system. The Federation denounced Hinduism as a system
by which Brahmans controlled the masses. Many D.K.
members were atheists who impugned such basic Hindu
concepts as transmigration and salvation.

The D.M.K. (*Dravida Muneetra Kazagham*, the Dravidian Progressive Federation) broke away from the D.K.
in 1949. The new movement was not secessionist, but
its members did appeal to regionalism and were eminent-
ly successful in 1967 in winning seats at all levels of
government in Tamilnadu. The D.M.K. was not so successful in 1972, but still it is a political movement of
some power. It is the only major political party explicitly anti-caste and composed of members almost entirely from one division of castes—the high Shudra
castes. Whether the D.M.K. will become a model for
future political parties is difficult to say.

DEMOCRACY IN INDIA

India has been an effective democracy since Independence from Britain in 1947. Since the 1880s, elections had been held for offices at various levels; but not until the nationwide elections of 1952 were *all* adults eligible to vote. Following the example of the Western democracies, electoral campaigns are waged by political parties, and winning elections has become a principal means of gaining power in modern India.

At first it appeared that caste block-voting would emerge as an important phenomenon, dominant castes transplanting their local rivalries and influence into the arena of state electoral politics. For example, during the elections of 1955 in Andhra Pradesh, two dominant peasant castes contended. One caste, the *Kammas*, supported the Communist Party; the other, the *Reddis*, supported the Congress Party (Harrison 1960).

The Caste Association. The caste association, a voluntary organization composed of members from a single caste, was also viewed by political scientists as a potentially important political instrument. The caste association could demand candidacies or concessions in return for support by the caste. Also, through the association the urban politically-literate elite were linked with the less literate villagers belonging to the same caste.

Caste associations linking members of a caste within a region first emerged in the nineteenth century. Such associations became possible as education became more accessible and easier means of communication and transportation were established (trains, roads, printing presses, a postal service). Often, the associations were funded by Western-educated male members. These organizations published newspapers and held conferences to discuss discrimination suffered, reform of customs, and the establishment of benefits such as scholarships and hostels (dormitories) for their student members.

Some caste associations have participated effectively in politics. Lloyd and Susanne Rudolph described the way in which the *Vanniya Kula Kshatrya Sangham*, a caste association in Northern Tamilnadu, was

able to support political parties and strike political
bargains resulting in their representation in the state
legislature in a relatively high number (Rudolph and
Rudolph 1960). However, subsequent studies of caste
associations seem to indicate that the political suc-
cesses of the Vanniya Kula Kshatrya Sangham were more
the exception than the rule. R. S. Khare's study of
the *Kanyakubja* Brahman association, for example, re-
vealed that this organization had not engaged "either
in any 'protective' or protest politics for mobility or
for modernization" (Khare 1970: 197).

A caste association must solve a number of problems if it is to be successful in politics. First,
the population is fragmented into so many castes that
even a dominant caste in a region does not constitute
a majority of the electorate. Second, few castes are
organized adequately to mobilize all members of the
caste to vote as a block. An association's ability to
deliver the vote can be undermined rather easily by
the opposition parties' putting up candidates from the
same caste. André Béteille notes that in Tanjore District, Tamilnadu, where the largest caste is the *Kallas*, all parties put up Kalla candidates (Béteille
1970: 266). Such techniques tend to defeat the power
of the caste association as a political organization.
Since it is narrowly identified with one caste, the
organization cannot attract the support of voters of
other castes unless it abolishes its exclusiveness and
thus ceases to be a caste association.

THREE STAGES IN THE RELATIONSHIP BETWEEN CASTE AND
POLITICS

Rajni Kothari, a political scientist, has specified
three typical stages in the relationship between caste
and politics in a region.

Stage 1: This involves the politicization of a
powerful elite caste, usually one which responded
earliest to the opportunities for Western education.
In Maharashtra and Tamilnadu, this was the Brahmans; in
Bihar, it was the *Kayesthas* (traditionally scribes) (Roy
1970: 239). With some political success on the part of
the entrenched caste, the members of other high castes

in the area would respond with resentment, feelings of relative deprivation, and possibly antagonism. These castes then challenge the entrenched caste as what Kothari calls an "ascendant caste." In three examples given in Kothari's edited book, the ascendant caste is one of respectable cultivators who had been slower than the entrenched caste in accepting Western education. In Rajasthan, the Rajputs were the entrenched, and the Jat cultivators the ascendant caste (Sisson 1970). In Tamilnadu, the Brahmans were the entrenched, and the Shudra non-Brahmans were ascendant (Béteille 1970: 260); and in Maharashtra, the Brahmans were the entrenched, and the Marathas were the ascendant (Rosenthal 1970: 355).

Stage 2: Factionalism and fragmentation take place within the competing castes, and multi-caste and multifactional alignments develop. Lower castes are often brought in to support high caste leaders and to strengthen a faction.

Stage 3: Caste identity tends to languish with the progress in education, urbanization, and the development of an orientation toward individual achievement and modern status symbols. Individuals participate in networks which include persons of several castes. In Kothari's words, "The structure of particularistic loyalties" has been "overlaid by a more sophisticated system of social and political participation with crosscutting allegiances. Institutional differentiation and specialization has progressed, so that economic, political, educational institutions are distinctly different" (Kothari 1970: 20-23).

The Indian sociologist, G. S. Ghurye, raised the spectre of a future with Indian society fixed in Stage 2—composed of a few blocks or coalitions of castes. This could occur through the gradual breakdown of rules of exogamy between castes of neighboring rank, so that each connubium was enlarged to include several castes of adjoining rank. If this happened, the French social anthropologist, Louis Dumont, sees a result that:

> would be disastrous, for one would end up by aggregating a multitude of small groups into a few

large blocks, which would be mutually hostile and exclusive to a dangerous degree.

(Dumont 1970: 222)

Dumont believes that such blocks of castes would not be ranked or interdependent, but would be, rather:

a universe of impenetrable blocks, self-sufficient, essentially identical and in competition with one another.

(*Ibid.*)

Whether Ghurye's or Kothari's vision is correct is hard to say. Kothari suggests that identifications other than that of caste are likely to become more important with advancing education, urbanization, and adoption of a modern achievement-orientation (Stage 3). André Béteille has pointed out, for example, that among the westernized elite, school-ties are much more important than caste ties (Béteille 1969: 209-210). Salient identifications do not accumulate and crystallize in the modern sector as they did in the traditional. In the India of today, all of an individual's relationships are not channeled in caste grooves.

The D.M.K. party in Tamilnadu is the only important political phenomenon resembling such a block of castes as Dumont speaks of. The party is composed of many members of the high Shudra castes and is explicitly anti-Brahman. The Republican Party is composed very largely of Untouchable Mahars of Maharashtra, but it includes other Untouchables in central and northern India. It has not yet wielded much political power.

A process of fusion of castes resulting in only a few contending caste blocks could take place only if other bases of alignment between people, families, and groups were consistently in abeyance—a rather unlikely condition. If all castes were distributed among a few major blocks contending for power through election and governmental institutions, there would be a new caste system based on a principle of competition.

DEMOCRACY AND THE INDIAN VILLAGE

So far caste and politics have been discussed in terms of higher, national government levels. How has democracy in India affected village elections?

Throughout India, elected village and district governing institutions were introduced by the 1960s. Elections to such local *panchayats* (councils) are often tensely contested. Large landless castes now have the power of voting strength, so they may and sometimes do challenge the traditionally-dominant caste which has power derived from land control. Dominant castes as well as ascendant castes are usually tied in with the important political parties of a region, and upward mobility through the political party organization takes place. The most talented men desert the village political arenas for the larger arenas at district, state, and national levels. Sometimes local rivalries are projected onto wider stages (Johnson 1973). Within localities, elected leaders often displace the hereditary caste headmen and other traditional leaders in the performance of such duties as the settlement of disputes, leadership in village ceremonial events, and other undertakings.

Chapter 10

Untouchability and the Government

Traditional Hindu law, as expressed in the various
Dharmashastras, systematically graded punishments and
privileges according to *varna* (social class category).*
Thus Brahmans' crimes were punished less severely than
were those of Kshatriyas, whose crimes were punished
less than those of Vaishyas, and so on. During the
British period, that tradition was displaced by a principle of equality of all before the law. However, this
principle was accompanied by a British policy of non-
interference in caste affairs and little attempt at reform. The courts did not punish a caste for boycotting
another, or for ordering a servant caste to boycott
others. A caste could outcast its members without
overrule by the court. Courts even upheld caste by
issuing injunctions prohibiting lower castes from en-
tering temples, and awarding damages for purificatory
ceremonies after lower caste persons had "polluted" a
sanctuary. Even reformers working against the abuses
of the caste system received no protection from the
courts. As the legal scholar, Marc Galanter, observed:

> the criminal law was interpreted to give a broad
> immunity to the efforts of higher castes to keep
> lower castes in their place.
>
> (Galanter 1972: 234)

Reformers and politicians did not become concerned
about Untouchability until the early twentieth century.
Indeed, the term "Untouchable" was first used by the

*See pages 31-35.

126

Maharaja of Baroda before the Depressed Classes Mission
of Bombay in 1909 (Galanter 1972: 298).

TWO LEADERS WHO FOUGHT FOR BETTERMENT OF UNTOUCHABLES

Two leaders fought for the betterment of Untouchables.
The first, M. K. Gandhi, emerged as a leader of the
nationalist movement; and he linked the eradication of
Untouchability, as well as unity between Hindus and
Muslims, with the goal of independence from Britain.
The other, himself a Mahar Untouchable, educated at
Columbia University, was Bhimrao Ramji Ambedkar.
     The goals of the two men differed. Gandhi's aim
was to absorb the Untouchables into the Shudra varna
and for all "caste Hindus" to treat them with respect;
in his ideal world of the future, he would have maintained the four varnas, but all would be of equal rank
and worth in society. Ambedkar, on the other hand,
wanted education, political power, and high position in
the modern sector for Untouchables; he was against the
entire caste system.
     The two men also disagreed about the role of the
Untouchables in the modern Indian democratic society
about to be established. Ambedkar wanted separate
electorates so that Untouchables could elect their own
representatives from among themselves. The Muslims had
made such a demand, and Ambedkar could see its advan-
tage as a device for attaining political power. Gandhi
argued that separate electorates would perpetuate the
category of Untouchables instead of encouraging them to
merge with the Shudra population; he feared conflict
between "caste Hindus" and Untouchables.
     In 1932, Gandhi began a fast to protest the award
of separate electorates to Untouchables. Ambedkar
bowed to this pressure, giving up his demand for separate electorates in return for a much higher number of
seats in Parliament *reserved* for Untouchables. The
number of reserved seats was made proportionate to the
number of Untouchables in the total population (12.5%).
The occupants of such reserved seats were elected by
the total voting population, not by an electorate of
Untouchables alone. This arrangement continues today.
One in seven seats in central and state legislatures
is occupied by an Untouchable representative.

In the 1920s, both Gandhi and Ambedkar worked for the opening of Hindu temples to low-caste worshippers. Their efforts were rewarded by a large number of bills passed in central and state legislatures and, in princely states, by the opening of temples to all and the protection of low castes from various disabilities. More such acts were passed after the Second World War (Zelliot 1972).

"PROTECTIVE DISCRIMINATION"

The term "Scheduled Castes," by which Untouchables are also called, refers to a list of castes prepared in 1935 by the British government in India. Such a list is kept today, supplemented by lists of Scheduled Tribes and Backward Classes. All of these groups are beneficiaries of "protective discrimination," a term applied to the laws reserving seats in legislatures, government employment, places in schools and universities, as well as provisions for certain financial assistance for Scheduled Castes (Dushkin 1972: 176). Dushkin concludes from her assessment of these programs that, in spite of them, Untouchables still lag behind the rest of the population in literacy. Thus, in 1961, only 10.3 percent of Untouchables were counted as literate as compared to 24 percent in the total population. The proportion of Scheduled Caste persons in government white-collar positions, also, is far below the reserved percentages (Dushkin 1972).

The Constitution of India of 1950 abolishes Untouchability and prohibits discrimination in "access to shops, public restaurants, hotels and places of entertainment," or in "use of wells, tanks, bathing ghats, roads, and places of public resort," or in admission to educational institutions. Article 23 forbids forced labor, commonly part of the dominant caste rule or feudal regime. Article 25 allows for entrance to Hindu religious institutions. In addition to these protections in the Constitution, in 1955 the Parliament passed the Untouchability (Offences) Act.

Galanter found that very few cases have ever been brought under the Untouchability (Offences) Act, and of those, few have been decided in favor of the Untouchables. Of the 476 taken by the *Harijan Sevak*

Sangh (The Service Society for the Children of God—
i.e., Untouchables) between 1961 and 1966, only 90
cases (19 percent) resulted in convictions; and the
median fine in such cases was ten rupees (a little
over one dollar). As Galanter concludes: "It is,
simply, very hard to win one of these cases" (Galanter
1972: 278). He believes that legislation protecting
Untouchables could be improved and that other kinds of
initiatives could be taken by the government to seek
out "patterns of discrimination." However, he says:
"There is no interest in the intellectual community in
the mechanics of programs for attacking untouchability,
no debate about alternatives, no assessment of prospects" (*Ibid.*: 276).

However, because such legislation exists, other
Hindus often assume that Untouchables are doing very
well, and indeed are getting ahead at the expense of
caste Hindus.

In her assessment of Untouchable political power
through the "reserved seats" in Parliament, Dushkin
found that control of the Untouchables' one-seventh of
the electorate is often important to a candidate. In
1967, when Indira Gandhi's return as Prime Minister was
accomplished by a very narrow margin of votes, there
were enough Congressmen holding reserved seats to have
"brought down the government." Their support of Mrs.
Gandhi was rewarded by various legislation favoring
Untouchables (Dushin 1972).

RELIGIOUS CONVERSION AND DEFECTION FROM HINDUISM

A major threat which Untouchables used from time to
time is defection from Hinduism, for it implies independence from, defiance of the control by upper-caste
Hindus. For example, the temple entry proclamation of
1936 in the religiously conservative princely state of
Travancore was the culmination of a movement begun in
1921 when the sizeable Irava Untouchable caste threat-
ened to convert to Christianity (Zelliot 1972: 79). In
the past, Untouchables have converted to Islam, Christianity, and Sikhism. Usually, however, they have continued to be considered Untouchables by Hindus. The
latest, most dramatic movement has been the conversion

of millions of Central and North Indian Untouchables to Buddhism.

Ambedkar and Buddhism. As noted earlier, Ambedkar had worked for temple-entry for Untouchables in the 1920s. He had made other efforts also to Sanskritize Mahar caste life (Zelliot 1966: 196; Zelliot 1970: 37; Patwardhan 1973: 124, 139), but in 1935, he declared, "I was born in the Hindu religion; but I will not die in the Hindu religion" (Zelliot 1966: 199-200). There was speculation over the years that Ambedkar might convert either to Sikhism or to Islam. In fact, in Nagpur, on October 14, 1956, he converted to Buddhism. This occurred in the presence of hundreds of thousands of Mahar Untouchables, most of whom also underwent conversion.

Ambedkar wrote *The Buddha and his Dhamma* as a guide for the Mahars, "a secular rational social interpretation of Buddhism" (Zelliot 1966: 203). He rejected some of the basic tenets of Buddhism such as the four Noble Truths concerning suffering and the requirement of Renunciation. He was not attracted by philosophical or mystical Buddhism, but Ambedkar liked Buddha's insistence that he was not divine, that his teachings were not revelations but discoveries by man. Patwardhan says, "It was the moral bases of equality, justice, and wide humanitarianism that attracted him (Ambedkar) to Buddhism" (Patwardhan 1973: 138). Ambedkar also preferred Buddhism to Islam or Christianity, because it was a religion of Indian origin; yet, like Islam and Christianity, Buddhism is against the caste system.

Ambedkar saw Buddhism as an excellent alternative to communism for Untouchables. He pointed out that "Buddhism contained all of communism's economic and egalitarian benefits without communism's violent methods" (Zelliot 1966: 209-210). He also thought that Buddhism was a religion to which all of India could eventually turn (*Ibid.*: 209). The fact that Ambedkar rejected communism in favor of Buddhism has perhaps had immense effect on Indian politics.

In converting to Buddhism, the Untouchable rejected all Hindu gods and ritual. Most threw away their idols of Hindu deities and many gave up their lowly ritual duties in the *balūta* system of Maharashtra state, the

Maharashtrian equivalent of the North Indian jajmani
system. Since there is a dearth of leaders trained in
Buddhism, however, most new Buddhists continue to cele-
brate Hindu festivals and to perform life cycle rites
according to Hindu liturgy.

In converting to Buddhism, the individual makes
five moral affirmations which include refraining from
harm to living beings and abstention from theft, sexual
misconduct, wrong speech, and intoxicants (Zelliot
1966: 206).

In his study of the Untouchable Jatav Shoemakers
of the city of Agra in Uttar Pradesh where there were
many new Buddhists, Owen Lynch noted that their worship
centered more upon Ambedkar than upon Buddha. Thus,
important holidays celebrated included Ambedkar's
birthday and the anniversary of his death. Ambedkar's
birthday was the most important holiday (Lynch 1969:
151).

Ambedkar already headed a political party called,
first, the Independent Labor Party, and then renamed
the Scheduled Castes Federation. After his death in
1957, it became the Republican Party, composed again
almost entirely of Mahars. Some of the leaders of the
Buddhist order were also leaders in the Republican
Party, but there were Buddhist religious leaders who
were not so involved. Where a high proportion of the
population is Mahar, as in some localities in Maharashtra, the Republican Party has been successful in gaining office. However, its success otherwise has depended upon its uniting with other parties in coalitions.

THE NEW BUDDHISTS

It is estimated that 75 percent of the Mahars of Maharashtra have converted to Buddhism. The religion has
grown in other states as well—Madhya Pradesh, Panjab,
Uttar Pradesh, Andhra Pradesh, Gujarat, Kerala, Assam,
Bihar, and Madras (Patwardhan 1973: 126-127). In all
of India, the number of Buddhists increased from 180,
823 in 1951 to 3,250,227 in 1961; and most of the
growth is due to the conversion of Untouchables (Zelliot 1966: 191).

One of the problems for the new Buddhists is
whether to claim and to accept the special benefits
legally reserved for Hindu Untouchables. In Maharashtra, but not elsewhere, they have succeeded in insuring
these benefits (Zelliot 1966: 193). The Republican
Party has agitated for such benefits for Buddhists; it
has also demanded land for Untouchables, slum clear-
ance, and implementation of the Minimum Wage Act.

Zelliot reports that many of the Mahars themselves
say they experienced a new psychological freedom upon
conversion (Zelliot 1966: 205). As might be expected,
members of the higher castes of Hindus still consider
the new Buddhists to be Untouchables. Patwardhan records a number of newspaper reports of atrocities committed against new Buddhists—in part "punishment" for
the Buddhists' refusing to fulfill traditional Mahar
ritual duties such as sanitation work, carrying lan-
terns during high caste jajmans' weddings, and so on
(Zelliot 1966: 205).

Educated Buddhists have no problem getting employment since proportions of places in government are
reserved for Untouchables. This drainage of potential
leadership talent into government has weakened religious and political efforts in behalf of Untouchables
(Lynch 1969: 107).

There is no question that Untouchables are not
advancing as rapidly as the legislated quotas originally forecasted. Possibly, discrimination against Untouchables will persist long after the rules of pollution between other castes and caste segments have
disappeared. The Untouchables in India might, then,
take a place in society similar to Untouchable groups
in Japan and Korea, where small communities of Untouchables, once connected with occupations considered by
Buddhists to be violent—cobblers, leatherworkers,
fishermen—still persist as groups with whom the rest
of the population refuses to intermarry (Donoghue 1966).

Chapter 11

The Commercialization of Agriculture and the Release of Agrestic Laborers from the Caste System

Commercialization of agriculture commenced during the British period. Its effect, as it developed, was the release of large numbers of agricultural laborers from the caste system. The numbers of unemployed and landless have reached alarming proportions during recent decades. In this chapter the commercialization of agriculture upon the rural caste system are examined.

There is ample evidence, as discussed in Chapter 3, that the local caste system characterized by organic solidarity, as in the jajmani system and the hali system, is in decline. This is due to the great expansion in the scale of political and economic relations of the typical village. Such an increase was facilitated by the improved means of transportation and communication introduced over the past 150 years. Today, Indian villagers can go to town to work, and to buy and sell goods and services; their dependence upon the local dominant caste for work, and upon artisans and servants in a local jajmani system for goods and services has lessened.

The introduction of cash crops and better agricultural methods turns the landowner from subsistence agriculture to more capitalistic profit-maximizing agriculture. The introduction of national, state, and district democratic politics reorients the dominant castes and local elites, so they attend power ventures on a larger scale than the village and immediate locality.

The motivation of the dominant caste has changed over recent decades. As described earlier, the local caste system was developed and integrated by a protector caste. Sometimes the dominant caste was a set of tenants of a jagirdar, who was expected to protect villagers; sometimes the dominant caste members controlled the land directly. The willingness of lower castes to accept menial work and lowly rank can be understood as a trade-off between service on their side and protection on the side of the dominant caste or jagirdar. The dominant caste or officials were usually much less concerned about the yield of agricultural products from the land than they were about maintaining their power and territory; and, if possible, of extending that power and territory. They depended upon the members of other castes for support as retainers. Often, these petty rulers conceived of their duty as that of the ancient Kshatriya varna—to protect their people and to conquer surrounding peoples. Land had to be cultivated, of course, and many a ruler was panicked periodically by the desertion of the tillers from the land, due to oppressive taxation, famine, warfare, or unjust treatment. All in all, the traditional caste system was a kind of political arrangement, as well as division of labor in a subsistence economy, and a royal-priestly-oriented ritual structure.

THE BRITISH INTRODUCTION OF LAND OWNERSHIP

The British conquerors hoped that when law and order was established in their Indian empire, the land-controlling class would become rural entrepreneurs, interested in maximizing agricultural yields and improving their lands and agricultural methods. The British gave the ownership of the land to those who, previously, had been primarily tax collectors. As Walter Neale (1957: 225), Louis Dumont (1970), and Barrington Moore, Jr. (1966) have pointed out: In pre-British times, there were multiple claims on the village harvest. The central government's claim, as represented by the tax collector, was only one along with the claims of the lagdars, halis, *purohits*, and religious mendicants of a village. The British are often criticized for their misunderstanding of the Indian village economy and for their conversion of land into a commodity by giving land ownership to those who had previously merely represented the ruler's claim.

One of the effects of the rather rigorous land revenue system instituted by the British was the mortgaging of land as landholders, unable to pay their taxes, turned for help to moneylenders. Many mortgages were, of course, foreclosed. There was a great deal of land sale and a resultant concentration of landownership.

ATTEMPTS TO COMMERCIALIZE
INDIAN AGRICULTURE

An accompanying trend was toward an increasing number and proportion of agricultural workers. Surendra J. Patel has estimated that the proportion of landless and land-poor laborers in India increased from 13 percent of the rural population in 1891 to 38 percent in 1951 (Patel 1952, cited in Moore 1966: 368). Such population shifts are to be expected during the modernization of agriculture; but, in fact, modernization of agriculture in India has been very slow. Blyn has shown that during the latter part of the nineteenth century and the first half of the twentieth century, agricultural output in India was growing at an average rate of less than a half of one percent per year, with food-grain yields increasing at an even lesser rate (only .11 percent per year). At the same time, the population was growing .67 percent per year (Blyn 1966, cited by Joshi 1974: 182).

Under British rule, the large landholders did not become squire-entrepreneurs. They continued to be willing to settle for a rather low yield, provided they could leave the actual labor on the land to lower castemen and not have to supervise workers themselves. The traditional disdain for manual work on the part of the twice-born accounts, in part, for this attitude; but there were other factors involved as well. The stimulus from cities in the form of a demand for raw materials or for capital for investment in industry was weak in British India. A segment of "modern-style" businessmen interested in machine-powered industry did develop in the second half of the nineteenth century. Also, a modest plantation economy in the Southwest and Northeast was established. However, the overall stimulus from the commercial classes of the city to the landholders to produce higher yields was weak.

As Barrington Moore, Jr. has pointed out, the rather slow rate of economic development in India can be accounted for by a vicious circle: The modern commercial class was small in number and, therefore, unable to stimulate very greatly the rural cultivators to produce more crops. Such stimulation might have taken the form of higher prices for produce, or the attraction of manufactured goods that the food-producer was enticed to buy. As an alternative, the commercial bourgeoisie might themselves have become capitalistic farmers by buying up land; this actually has happened in some parts of India, such as Tamilnadu. The generally low yields meant that there was little agricultural surplus available to convert into capital for investment in industry; so, in turn, there was insignificant stimulus from the industrial city for higher yields—since there was little modern industry. Moore believes that the failure to channel the profit from surplus agricultural produce into industrial development is the main reason why India has been so slow to develop a modern machine-powered economy. He sees the caste system as a barrier to such development in that the system supports a low-yielding agriculture. This is due to the fact that Untouchables do most of the agricultural labor for largely parasitic landowners who take little interest in cultivation. Even in recent years, when the Indian government has had as part of its Community Development Program, a pan-Indian program for improvement in agricultural practices, the yields per land-unit have not improved very greatly. Consider, in contrast, the tremendous increase in rice production in Japan, for example, with the very modest increases in rice production in India. Kusum Nair, who has compared agriculture in Japan with that in India, points out that the average yield of rice per hectare in India in 1962 was half or less than that of Japan in 1882 (Nair 1969: 233).

Post-Independence Land Reforms. After Independence in 1947, land reform was slated for early enactment. P. C. Joshi has shown how the intent to introduce land reform, and the legislation actually established led to the further concentration of land in the hands of the larger landowners. Many of these are the dominant castemen so important in the operation of the caste system. To make his point, Joshi drew on studies from the areas of Andhra Pradesh, Maharashtra, Gujarat, and West Bengal—in other words, from a wide geographical range.

The original principle of land reform was "Land to the Tiller." Since a great deal of the land in India was rented to tenants, most land reform legislation provided that a tenant who had cultivated a piece of land for many years would now become the owner of that land.

The large landowners, anticipating this type of legislation, evicted long-term tenants prior to land reform enactments. In fact, such action on the part of landlords continued even after legislation was passed since the laws were not well enforced. The power situation was such that, in many instances, long-term tenants gave up their rights "voluntarily" out of fear of the landlord. Thereafter, the large landowner rented out his land to short-term or seasonal tenants; or tried to cultivate the best land himself with the aid of family members, day labor, or casual labor such as the migrant laborers intruding on the traditional hali rights of the Dublas (Breman 1974). Absentee landlords had a harder time retaining their land. In the end, the total effect of land reform measures was to strengthen the landed resident peasantry who were already the dominant caste in many localities. In some instances, peasant cultivators of middle-rank in the caste system who previously had been tenants of absentee landlords, often maharajas or jagirdars, became the owners, and thus became a more powerful dominant caste (Joshi 1974).

By 1953-54, the upper 10 percent of landowners owned more than half of the land, while 47.2 percent of rural households owned less than 1 acre per household, and 23.09 percent were landless. (National Sample Survey Report on Land Holding, cited by Nair 1969: 305-306). In 1963, it was estimated that the top 1 percent

of rural households owned 18 percent of the rural
wealth (National Council of Applied Economic Research
1965: 29). Leased land declined from 35.7 percent in
1950-51 to only 10.7 percent in 1961-62. Joshi emphasizes that this was *not* due to transfer of land to the
long-term tenant. Rather, the decrease reflects the
process of taking land back for self-cultivation by
owners, and the disappearance entirely of small tenants
(Joshi 1974: 333).

Although agricultural production was growing at a
rate of about 3 percent per year in the post-Independence period, economists see the government policies as
having failed to stimulate output during the 1960s
(Economic Research Unit of the Indian Statistical Institute 1975: 84). However, in some areas of India,
productivity increased during the late 1960s as part of
what has been called the "green revolution."

"The Green Revolution." "The green revolution" was a
term used for the expected increase in agricultural
productivity to be brought about by the introduction,
beginning in 1966, of high-yielding varieties of wheat,
rice, maize, sorghum, and millet (Nair 1969: 207).
Nair (1969), Frankel (1971), Byres (1972), and other
investigators found that the introduction of high-
yielding varieties benefited the larger landholder
more than the small landholder, or the landless laborer. The reasons for this are as follows: First, cultivation of high-yielding varieties requires a reliable supply of water and costly fertilizer, seed, and
pesticides. The additional expense meant that only
the richer farmers could afford to grow the high-
yielding varieties, especially given the inaccessibil-
ity of credit facilities to small farmers. Second,
some of the larger farmers began to use machinery in
place of hired agricultural labor—resulting in a
version of technological unemployment. Thus, the number of tractors in Punjab-Haryana, a high-yield wheat
area, increased from 8000 in 1961 to 25,000 in 1970
(Byres 1972: 107). Third, some landowners turned out
sharecroppers or tenants in order to cultivate the land
themselves—sometimes consolidating their holdings for
greater efficiency in tilling. Fourth, many larger
farmers changed their pattern of employment from more

traditional patronage relationships, such as the hali system, to a pattern of hiring a few skilled workers who could run and repair modern machinery. Some farmers rely heavily on family labor, hiring casual labor on a cash basis. The landholder's only obligation to such labor is the paying of wages.

P. C. Joshi has noted another new trend in the Panjab-Haryana high productivity areas. He calls it a reverse-tenantry-move, in which a small landowner rents his land—not to a poor, landless, or land-poor sharecropper—but to a commercial farmer who needs a larger landspread to use his machinery profitably (Joshi 1974: 33).

Note that these changes represent the moves by capitalist farmers. The landowner-as-entrepreneur that the British hoped for has finally arrived. However, one of the effects of the high-yielding varieties program has been the enrichment of the larger landholder and the increase in the numbers of landless laborers, most of whom are low-caste and Untouchable. Meanwhile, there has been no adequate program of employment for such disemployed in public works programs, or in agroindustries or urban-based industries. The influence which the dominant castemen tend to have in political parties means that such programs, as well as land legislation preventing excessive dispossession of tenants, are unlikely to be implemented. Furthermore, with respect to the needs for capital for investment, the taxation rate is too low for the central or state governments to channel some of the agrarian profits into investment in industry to employ the landless laborers (Byres 1972).

Kusum Nair has suggested that the upper 10 percent of landowners could probably produce enough food by means of high-yielding seeds, fertilizers, pesticides, and irrigation to feed the urban and other nonagricultural populations of India. Thus, it would be unnecessary for the other 90 percent of cultivators to invest in high-yielding crops. If the present trend were to continue, the more competent commercial producers could quickly buy out the small producers. Nair raises the dire spectre of 48 million families (15 million landless plus 33 million owning less than 5 acres per family), pushed off the land, with no alternative

means of livelihood. She points out that even the industrial complex of the United States, if transferred
to India, could not employ such a large number of
available workers (Nair 1969: 222-224).

The commercialization of agriculture, whether the
slow process that occurred during the 150 years of
British rule, or the more rapid process that has begun
in the last decade, spells the demise of patronage systems such as the jajmani and hali systems—those. networks of interdependence between the landed dominant
caste and its artisans, household servants, and agrestic servants. In the break-down of the caste system,
the fortune of the lowest groups is not necessarily
to come up in an equalizing process. They may, as current trends suggest, sink lower economically to become
rural unemployed. Their lot is likely to be worst in
the wheat-growing areas where extensive agricultural
operations requiring machinery are the most feasible
farming methods. In rice-growing areas where labor-
intensive methods of agriculture are appropriate, the
landless farm worker is less hard hit. (Migdal 1974:
153, 163; Frankel 1971; Byres 1972).

Chapter 12

Caste in the City

Relatively few Indians live in cities; thus, in 1971, only about 10 percent of the population lived in cities of over 100,000 (Census of India 1971: 3-6). The major cities—Bombay, Calcutta, and Madras—were founded as ports of the British East India Company. Many other cities, however, are much older; Delhi, for example, has been a capital of one regime or another for more than a thousand years (Rao and Desai 1965: 25).

The cultural patterns of the indigenous city were not distinctly different from those of the village. Instead of a dominant caste, a ruler and his coterie integrated a city. The ruler, of course, might be part of a regional dominant caste (Fox 1971). A ruler invited representatives of various castes to settle in his capital; and, in fact,the contingents of castes in cities were more complete than in villages—including more artisan, banking, and trading castes (Rowe 1973: 213, 220). "Compacts" or contracts describing the rights and obligations of caste contingents settling in a city were sometimes written. Some of these survive to the present (*Ibid.*: 218, 219, 223).

Jajmani relations also occurred and still occur in cities. Sylvia Vatuk, in her study of two white-collar workers' neighborhoods in Meerut in North India, composed mostly of Brahmans and Vaishya, found that families typically retained four servants: the Bhangi Sweeper, the Nāi Barber, the Kumhār Potter, and the

Brahman household priest. Payments to all were in
cash, not grain, although the Sweeper and Barber
women received daily and festival food, clothing, and
gifts at the time their children married. There were
certain modifications in these jajmani-type relations,
as compared to their village counterparts. The Bhangi
Sweeper considered herself attached to a house, rather
than to its occupants, and she served each renting family in turn. The jajmani work of the Nāi and of the
Potter were largely ritual, especially in connection
with weddings. The Nāi might have his own barber shop,
but he did not include barbering in his jajmani duties.
Similarly, the attachment to a Potter family was for
the sake of a ceremony at the Potter's wheel that takes
place during a marriage. Pottery was actually pur-
chased with cash by bargaining for each piece (Vatuk
1972: 156-160, 188).

There were, and are still in cities, caste wards
or quarters, governed by caste panchayats (councils).
The structure of monocaste quarters may be similar to
that of the traditional village caste enclave. Thus,
the Untouchable Jatavs of Agra, studied by Lynch, were
organized in a hierarchy of increasingly inclusive
panchayats, and neighborhoods had hereditary headmen.
In the early 1960s, however, both the panchayat system
and the hereditary headmanship tradition were in decline, because Jatav city officials, successful candidates in general city elections, also took over caste
community leadership (Lynch 1969). Similar displace-
ments are taking place today in villages. A man elected to the statutory panchayat of a village, or of a
set of villages, is also looked to as a leader of his
caste, both by outsiders and members of the caste.

In some caste quarters, as panchayats disappear,
they are replaced by caste associations (Patnaik 1960).
The leadership of these associations is in the hands of
the educated professional or commercial members of the
caste. Recently, multi-caste neighborhoods have developed, especially among white-collar workers in large
cities. Sometimes such communities lack organization
entirely; but usually occupants are of approximately
equal caste rank, and visiting and social relations
are likely to be limited to persons of approximately
equal caste rank (Vatuk 1972: 156).

MODERN INSTITUTIONS AND ORGANIZATIONS

The modern sector of contemporary Indian society is a series of institutions and organizations structured according to Western models, and located very largely in cities. These include universities, schools, scientific laboratories, hospitals, business firms, factories, national parliament, state legislative assemblies, government bureaus, political parties, military branches, and courts. Most of the institutions and organizations are structured in terms of a hierarchy of offices, but the principles of this hierarchy are not those of pollution and purity related to ritual, as in the traditional caste hierarchy. Rather, the new underlying principles are those of productivity, efficiency, coordination of effective activity, and maintenance of order—in other words, a rationalized bureaucratic hierarchy.

These modern organizations are not new on the Indian scene; Indians do not consider them to be foreign or un-Indian (Singer 1972: 392). However, a very small proportion of the population actually participates in them, and such participation is differentially distributed among different regional and caste groups. Thus, the coastal rimland of India (the States of Kerala, Maharashtra, Gujarat, Madras, West Bengal, Panjab) which includes the great ports of Madras, Calcutta, and Bombay tends to be considerably more modernized than the interior heartland of the sub-continent (the States of Bihar, Uttar Pradesh, Madhya Pradesh, Rajasthan) (Rudolph and Rudolph 1972: 52).

In the rimland, some castes had successful access to modern education and occupations earlier than did others. Around Poona and Bombay, the Chitpavan Brahmans, who had risen to power under the Maratha rulers, readily adopted English education, government jobs, and modern professions during the first half of the nineteenth century (Johnson 1973). Similarly, the Tamil Brahmans around Madras, and the "*Bhadralok*," (a group composed largely of high caste Brahmans, Kayasthas, and Vaidyas) around Calcutta, learned the English language earliest and became the middle-class aides of the British rulers (Broomfield 1968: 6-7). In some places, high castes, especially Brahmans, had a near monopoly on government jobs, as subordinates to British officials.

Envy of the Brahmans' near monopoly upon organization jobs in the modern sector probably accounts in large part for the anti-Brahman movements which developed in Maharashtra near Bombay in the mid-nineteenth century, and in Madras in the early twentieth century. Such movements were phrased in terms of the traditional oppression of the lower castes by the Brahmans, because of the latter's traditional claims of religious privileges and "purity." However, such movements had as principal goals the wresting of modern powers from Brahmans by limiting their numbers in government, universities, and businesses.

Since the passing of princely rule in India and the development of secondary urbanization along Western lines, there is no dominant caste or ruler in a city. Authority is fragmented, distributed among persons of a number of different castes. The jati, however, offers a ready-made organization to serve as a basis for business organization. A set of inter-marrying families may share capital, resources, and knowledge and feel constrained to cooperate as part of their kinship obligation (Fox 1973).

Harold Gould has spoken of the "ethnic cooptation" of modern occupations and professions that has sometimes taken place when one caste dominates a particular occupation (Gould 1973). An example is the Mahisyas, a Bengali cultivating caste, members of which have "coopted" engineering machine businesses in Howrah, near Calcutta. Raymond Owens found that Mahisya jati members hired each other as apprentices, workers, and partners. As a cultivating caste, Owens suggests, Mahisyas more readily entered a business requiring manual labor. Thus, there is for the Mahisyas a continuity between their traditional manual occupation and the modern manual occupation they have moved into (Owens 1973).

CASTE AND MODERN INDUSTRY

There are still rather few studies on the relationship between caste and modern industry. Those by Niehoff (1954), Lambert (1963), and Singer (1972) suggest a number of generalizations:

1. There is an assumption among the Indian public that employers give preference to members of their own caste in hiring, training, promotion, and contractual arrangements. Such assumptions have seldom been verified by systematically-collected sociological data, however.

2. Where there is a match between caste specialties and jobs in modern industry, there is some tendency for members of castes with such traditional occupations to fill the parallel positions. Thus, Blacksmiths, Carpenters, Potters, and especially Sweepers, Shoemakers, and Tanners find their traditional skills in demand and can transfer them to modern industry. Clean-caste Hindus will not do the "filthy" work of Sweepers, and few will defile themselves by working with raw leather.

3. Most jobs in modern industry are new in content and method, and since most are viewed as "ritually neutral," persons of any caste, including Untouchables and Brahmans, may fill them.

4. If factories require educated personnel, then disproportionate numbers of persons of the higher-castes who have taken to Westernized education earliest and with most success are likely to be employed.

5. Since there is a shortage of persons who speak English and of technically- and scientifically-educated persons, any caste preference in hiring must take second place to the requirement for such trained capacities.

6. Two strata appear to be emerging within Indian industry, parallel to the Blue-collar/White-collar division in Western industry. The two strata are drawn along boundaries of greater and less education, although the distinction may also be seen to replicate the old division between nonmanual and manual labor.

Benerally, the indications are that caste monopolies over special occupations, and the various facets of the Hindu pollution complex are increasingly irrelevant within the modern sector. To use Milton Singer's term, most of modern public life is "ritually neutral."

Hindu men are not much concerned about pollution from contact with lower-caste persons in city streets, in buses or trains, in office, factory, or shop. In factory or university canteens, there is little concern about persons of different caste eating together. In schools, children of high and low caste sit side-by-side. Both Milton Singer and Edward Shils have noted the tendency for men to *compartmentalize* their home context from work context. Traditional customs, including rules of purity and pollution, may be followed in the home; but they are largely ignored at work. (Shils 1960; Singer 1972).

PRACTICE OF RELIGION IN THE CITY

The member of a high caste may satisfy his religious conscience by financing religious readings or ceremonies which he does not have the time to perform or to attend himself. Singer calls this "vicarious ritualization." Thus, the traditional religious rituals are modernized—by being performed efficiently by a specialist all alone.

The most popular kind of religious activity is devotional—a much easier path to salvation than meditation or elaborate rituals. Urban devotional groups are likely to be composed of a number of different, clean Hindu castes (they exclude Untouchables). The ideal of equality in these religious activities is acclaimed. Brahmans working in the modern sector no longer devote years to the study of Sanskritic religious texts. A *democratization of Hinduism* is taking place via the radio and cinema. Thus the lower castes can no longer be prohibited from having contact with the Great Tradition of Hinduism (Singer 1972).

Individual Identity. Bopegamage and Veeraraghavan (1967) suggest that caste identity is not so prominent for an individual in the city as it is in the village. They studied two areas, one near the Central Indian city of Poona, and one near the South Indian manufacturing city of Coimbatore. In rural communities, villagers said, "I am a Mahar," or "I am a Vellala,"— choosing their caste membership for prime identity. In both cities, people did not readily identify themselves

by caste. When asked, "Who are you?" they answered by
occupation—"I am a factory worker," or "I am a stenog-
rapher"; or they answered by name—"I am a Kali Ram,"
"I am Dharam Singh" (Bopegamage and Veeraraghavan 1967:
41-42).

Gerald Berreman found also that in urban social
interaction caste identities form only part of their
referents. Regional origin, religion, occupation, and
urban or rural style were more often the key identities
focused upon (Berreman 1972b).

ROLE OF THE KIN-COMMUNITY IN MODERN INDIA

The kin-community is the large-scale descent-group released from the organic solidarity of the traditional
caste system. The kin-community is the large-scale
descent-group as it interfaces with the modern sector
of Indian society in which occupations are, at the
least, not normatively caste-related. In the modern
sector, castes usually do not have monopolies over
specified services or occupations, although in the
transition from traditional to modern organization instances of "ethnic cooptation" may develop!

The kin-community continues to be a connubium at
the appropriate endogamous levels of segmentation.
Members, born into it, marry into permissible segments
within the large-scale descent-group. Depending upon
the degree of westernization, the kin-community may
also be an ethnic group or sub-cultural group having
certain unique customs. In relation to the political,
economic, and educational institutions of the modern
secular sector of Indian society, the kin-community
functions primarily as a supplier of competent personnel. The descent-group serves as a resource network
for kin-community members seeking access to the modern
occupational structure. While such a network of
"brothers" usually functions largely on an informal
basis, some kin-communities do have voluntary organizations or even political parties associated with them.
Such organizations are typically composed of modern-
sector participants who try to advance the welfare of
the kin-community through contacts and exchanges with
schools and universities and with the government at

various levels. The kin-community and its associated
interest groups compete with other interest groups for
political power, job training, and job placement. De-
sirable jobs might be in schools, universities, businesses, factories, or government offices—all corporate
or institutional bodies organized according to Western
rationalistic principles of hierarchy and division of
labor directed toward efficient production. Contrast
these modern goals with the former organization according to Hindu principles of hierarchy and division of
labor for an enactment of a sacred order.

Conclusion

Few, if any, castes in India are entirely modernized. A single caste extending over a region usually includes within it segments that still operate within the traditional caste systems, and others which are modernized. There is one study which examines such diverse structures within the same caste, Robert Hardgrave's study, *The Nadars of Tamilnad* (Hardgrave 1969). However, the great diversity in the degree of modernization within the same endogamous unit is generally recognized by Indians themselves, as well as by anthropologists. Not only do segments within a jati differ in degree of modernization; but the segments, families, and lineages within a jati may have members in both traditional caste relations and in modern occupations. With seasonal migration, individuals may even move back and forth between the two (Breman 1974).

As previously defined in this book, those networks within a caste which are related to the modern sector are a kin-community. The kin-community may or may not be organized as a voluntary association. R. S. Khare's book, the *New Brahmans*, describes the kin-community of the Kanyakubja Brahmans which is organized as a caste association with a newspaper and annual meetings. The primary purpose of such an organization appears to be the maintenance of the connubium and the maintenance of the caste's subculture and sense of identity. It does not have any important political activities (Khare 1970).

On the other hand, educated caste members with modern occupations may organize as a pressure group or even a political party. As such, a caste association can compete as a corporate body with other pressure groups for political and economic resources. This type of organization represents a new kind of solidarity, a competitive equilibrium such as that sometimes said to characterize American political and economic life. Needless to say, the competing units need not be caste structures. They could be based on other solidarities—regional, linguistic, professional, or social class.

If group members are dispersed throughout a modern occupational structure which selects individuals according to competitive rules of meritocracy, should the descent-group continue to be called a caste? Some anthropologists, E. R. Leach (1960), Frederick Bailey (1963), and Richard Fox (1967) suggest that there is only a caste *system* when there is cooperation and interdependence between segments of different castes. If this explanation is accepted, can castes released from a *system* still be considered castes?

In this book the position taken is that in Indian thought, the caste is a *species* of mankind; thus both the term *casta* (from Portuguese used to translate the Indian term) and the Indian term itself (*jāti*), have that connotation. There does not appear to be any connotation in the terms that the relationships between these "species" must be cooperative. Such relationships could be competitive; and, presumably, the species could be isolated from one another and have no interrelationships. They could be independent from one another, and merely "co-exist."

During the period of organic solidarity, when there was a cooperative caste system, castes tended to fission, as sub-sections wished to gain a higher status than their caste-fellows through Sanskritization, or through obtaining wealth or power. Under a system of competitive solidarity the reverse occurs, and processes of fusion of sub-castes and fusion of castes tend to take place. Three kinds of fusion can be identified:

On the job and in newer neighborhoods, persons of different sub-castes and of different castes meet; they are usually of approximately equal caste rank. Neighborhood or office group solidarity (Khare 1973) develops. Broomfield points out that the barriers between the top three castes in Bengal were lowered during the nineteenth century because they shared government jobs and came to form inter-caste social groups (Broomfield 1968: 15).

Second, inter-sub-caste marriage takes place— promoting a fusion of sub-castes. Thus, it may be especially difficult to find a sufficiently educated bridegroom for an educated daughter within her own sub-caste, but one might be found in a neighboring sub-caste. However, few marriages between *ritually-distant* castes take place as yet.

Third, democratic politics foster the fusion of sub-castes and of adjacent castes in order for parties of substantial size to form. A prime example is the D.M.K. party of Tamilnadu, composed of members of higher non-Brahman (Shudra) castes.

In all three stages, the basic social segment has been the endogamous descent-group, the kinship nature of which has changed less than its ritual, economic, and political functions. The descent-group structure has persisted although its functions have differed in the contexts first of mechanical solidarity, then of organic solidarity, then of competitive solidarity.

The thesis of this book is that the persistent feature of Indian society, its basic building block, is the *endogamous descent-group*. Over time, such endogamous descent-groups were integrated into local hierarchical ritualized politico-economic systems of cooperation and interdependence. This cooperative caste system has broken down or is breaking down with the introduction of democracy and the integration of rural localities into regional, national, and international economies. A new system of competitive descent-groups is emerging as modern economic benefits and political power are prizes to be won rather than inheritances ascribed by birth. In the political and economic spheres of modern Indian life, ascribed rights are being replaced by goals achieved through competitive achievement. Yet the descent-group persists in modern India, although the system is a segmentary one, rather than an organic one.

References

Ahmad, Imtiaz (1973). "Introduction." In Imtiaz Ahmad, ed., *Caste and Social Stratification Among the Muslims*. Delhi: Manohar Book Service.

Alexander, K. C. (1975). "Some Characteristics of the Agrarian Social Structure of Tamilnadu." *Economic and Political Weekly* 10: 664-667.

Allchin, Bridget and Raymond (1968). *The Birth of Indian Civilization*. Hammondsworth, Middlesex, England: Penguin Books.

Anderson, Robert T. (1971). *Traditional Europe*. Belmont, California: Wadsworth Publishing Company, Inc.

Appadurai, Arjun and Carol Appadurai Breckenridge (1976). "The South Indian Temple: Authority, Honor and Redistribution," *Contributions to Indian Sociology* (forthcoming).

Arensberg, Conrad M. (1960). "The American Family in the Perspective of Other Cultures." In Eli Ginsberg, ed., *The Nation's Children, 1: Family and Social Change*. Washington, D.C.: White House Conference.

B. M. (1977). "Redefining Poverty." *Economic and Political Weekly* February 1977 Annual Number: 165-166.

Bailey, F. G. (1957). *Caste and the Economic Frontier*. Manchester, England: Manchester University Press.

Bailey, F. G. (1960). *Tribe, Caste, and Nation*. Manchester, England: Manchester University Press.

Bailey, F. G. (1963). "Closed Social Stratification in India." In *European Journal of Sociology* Volume IV, No. 1, 107-124.

Baines, J. A. (1912). *Ethnography, Castes and Tribes*. Strassburg: Karl J. Trubner.

Barber, Bernard (1957). *Social Stratification*. New York: Harcourt, Brace and World.

Barber, Bernard (1968). "Social Mobility in Hindu India." In James Silverberg, ed., *Social Mobility in the Caste System in India. Comparative Studies in Society and History*, Supplement III. Hague and Paris: Mouton.

Barnett, Stephen Alan (1970). "The Structural Position of a South Indian Caste: Kontaikkatti Velalars." Ph.D. Dissertation in Anthropology, University of Chicago.

Barth, Fredrik (1960). "The System of Social Stratification in Swat, North Pakistan." In E. R. Leach, ed., *Aspects of Caste in South India, Ceylon and North-West Pakistan*. Cambridge: University of Cambridge Press, 113-146.

Basham, A. L. (1954). *The Wonder that Was India*. New York: Grove Press.

Beals, Alan R. and Bernard J. Siegel (1966). *Divisiveness and Social Conflict*. Stanford: Stanford University Press.

Beck, Brenda E. F. (1972). *Peasant Society in Konku*. Vancouver: University of British Columbia Press.

Beck, Brenda E. F. (1976). "Centers and Boundaries of Regional Caste Systems: Toward a General Model." In Carol Smith, ed., *Regional Analysis* Volume II. New York/San Francisco/London: Academic Press. 255-288.

Begley, Vimla (1975). "Lecture on the Indus Valley Civilization." Houston Archeological Society, April 15, 1975.

Beidelman, T. O. (1959). *A Comparative Analysis of the Jajmani System*. Monograph of the Association for Asian Studies VII. Locust Valley, New York: J. J. Augustin.

Berreman, Gerald D. (1962). "Caste and Economy in the Himalayas." *Economic Development and Cultural Change* 10: 386-394.

Berreman, Gerald D. (1963). *Hindus of the Himalayas*. Berkeley and Los Angeles: University of California Press.

Berreman, Gerald D. (1964). "Brahmins and Shamans in Pahari Religion." *Journal of Asian Studies* 23: 53-69.

Berreman, Gerald D. (1966). "Caste in Cross-Cultural Perspective." In G. DeVos and H. Wagatsuma, eds., *Japan, Invisible Race: Caste in Culture and Personality*. Berkeley: University of California Press: 275-324.

Berreman, Gerald D. (1967a). "Caste as Social Process." *Southwestern Journal of Anthropology* 23: 351-370.

Berreman, Gerald. (1967b). "Stratification, Pluralism and Interaction: A Comparative Analysis of Caste." In A. V. S. de Reuck and Julie Knight, eds., *Caste and Race: Comparative Approaches*. London: J. & A. Churchill Ltd., 45-73.

Berreman, Gerald D. (1972a). "Race, Caste and Other Invidious Distinctions in Social Stratification," *Race*, April 1972, Vol. XIII, No. 4: 385-414.

Berreman, Gerald D. (1972b). "Social Categories and Social Interaction in a North Indian City," *American Anthropologist* 74: 567-586.

Berreman, Gerald D. (1973). *Caste in the Modern World*. Morristown, N.J.: General Learning Press.

Béteille, André (1969). *Castes: Old and New*. Bombay: Asia Publishing House.

Béteille, André (1970). "Castes and Political Group Formation in Tamilnad." In Rajni Kothari, ed., *Caste in Indian Politics*. New Delhi: Orient Longman Ltd.

Béteille, André (1971). "The Social Framework of Agriculture." In Louis Lefeber and Mrinal Datta Chaudhuri, eds., *Regional Development Experiences and Prospects in South and Southeast Asia*. The Hague/Paris: Mouton.

Blunt, E. A. H. (1969). *The Caste System of Northern India*. Delhi: S. Chand & Co. (Originally published in 1931.)

Blyn, George (1966). *Agricultural Trends in India, 1891-1947: Output, Availability and Productivity*. Philadelphia: University of Pennsylvania Press.

Bopegamage, A. and P. V. Veeraraghavan (1967). *Status Images in Changing India*. Bombay: Manaktalas.

Bose, Nirmal Kumar (1971). *Tribal Life in India*. New Delhi: National Book Trust.

Bouglé, Célestin (1971). *Essays on the Caste System*. Cambridge: Cambridge University Press. (Originally published in French in 1908.)

Brass, Paul R. (1973). "Political Parties of the Radical Left in South Asian Politics." In Paul R. Brass and Marcus F. Franda, eds., *Radical Politics in South Asia*. Cambridge, Massachusetts: MIT Press.

Breman, Jan (1974). *Patronage and Exploitation*. Berkeley: University of California Press.

Briggs, George W. (1920). *The Chamars*. London: Oxford University Press.

Broomfield, J. H. (1968). *Elite Conflict in a Plural Society*. Berkeley and Los Angeles: University of California Press.

Byres, T. J. (1972). "The Dialectic of India's Green Revolution." *South Asian Review* Vol. 5, No. 2, Jan. 1972, 99-116.

Census of India 1971. Paper of 1971-Supplement: Provisional Population.

Catanach, I. J. (1966). "Agrarian Disturbances in Nineteenth Century India." *Indian Economic and Social History Review* 3: 65-84.

Chakravarti, Anand (1976). *Contradiction and Change: Emerging Patterns of Authority in a Rajasthan Village*. New York: Oxford University Press.

Chaudhuri, S. B. (1955). *Civil Disturbances During the British Rule in India 1765-1857*. Calcutta: World Press.

Chaudhuri, S. B. (1957). *Civil Rebellion in the Indian Mutinies 1857-1859*. Calcutta: World Press.

Chauhan, Brij Raj (1967). *A Rajasthan Village*. New Delhi: Vir Publishing House.

Childe, V. Gordon (1953). *New Light on the Most Ancient East*. New York: Grove Press, Inc.

Cohn, Bernard S. (1968). "Notes on the History of the Study of Indian Society and Culture." In Milton Singer and Bernard S. Cohn, eds., *Structure and Change in Indian Society*. Chicago: Aldine Publishers, 1-25.

Correspondent (1974). "Attack on Dalit Panthers." *Economic and Political Weekly*, January 19, 1974: 51-52.

Crooke, William (1896). *Tribes and Castes of the North-Western Provinces and Oudh*. 4 volumes. Calcutta: Office of the Superintendent of Government Printing.

Dasgupta, Biplab (1974). *The Naxalite Movement*. Bombay: Allied Publishers.

Davis, Kingsley (1951). *The Population of India and Pakistan*. Princeton, N.J.: Princeton University Press.

Davis, Kingsley (1962). "Urbanization in India: Past and Future." In Roy Turner, ed., *India's Urban Future*. Berkeley and Los Angeles: University of California Press, 2-26.

Davis, Marvin (1976). "A Philosophy of Hindu Rank from Rural West Bengal." *Journal of Asian Studies* 36: 5-24.

DeBary, William, *et al.* (compilers) 1958. *Sources of Indian Tradition*. New York: Columbia University Press.

Donoghue, John (1967). "The Social Persistence of Outcaste Groups." In George DeVos and Hiroshi Wagatsuma, eds., *Japan's Invisible Race*. Berkeley and Los Angeles: University of California Press, 138-152.

Doshi, Harish (1974). *Traditional Neighborhood in a Modern City*. New Delhi: Abhinav Publications.

Dube, S. C. (1955). *Indian Village*. London: Routledge and Kegan Paul Ltd.

Dumont, Louis (1957a). "Hierarchy and Marriage Alliance in South Indian Kinship." *Occasional Papers of the Royal Anthropological Institute of Great Britain and Ireland*. No. 12.

Dumont, Louis (1957b). *Une Sous-Caste de l'Inde Du Sud*. Paris: Mouton.

Dumont, Louis (1959). "Pure and Impure": *Contributions to Indian Sociology* III: 9-39.

Dumont, Louis (1966). "The 'Village Community' From Munro to Maine." *Contributions to Indian Sociology* IX: 67-89.

Dumont, Louis (1970). *Homo Hierarchicus*. Chicago: University of Chicago Press. (Originally published in French in 1966.)

Dumont, Louis (1970a). *Religion, Politics, and History in India*. The Hague and Paris: Mouton.

Durkheim, Emile (1947). *The Division of Labor*. Glencoe, Illinois: Free Press. (Originally published in French in 1893.)

Durkheim, Emile (1951). *Suicide*. Glencoe, Illinois: Free Press. (Originally published in French in 1897.)

Durkheim, Emile (1915). *The Elementary Forms of the Religious*. London: George Allen and Unwin Ltd.

Dushkin, Lelah (1972). "Scheduled Caste Politics." In
J. Michael Mahar, ed., *The Untouchables in Contemporary India*. Tucson: University of Arizona Press.

Economic Research Unit of the Indian Statistical Institute (1975). "Structural Causes of the Economic
Crisis." *Economic and Political Weekly*, Jan. 18,
1975, 83-86.

Elder, Joseph W. (1970). "Rajpur: Change in the Jaj-
mani System of an Uttar Pradesh Village." In K.
Ishwaran, ed., *Change and Continuity in India's
Villages*. New York and London: Columbia University
Press.

Elliott, Carolyn M. (1970). "Caste and Faction Among
the Dominant Caste: The Reddis and Kammas of Andhra."
In Rajni Kothari, ed., *Caste in Indian Politics*.
Delhi: Orient Longman Ltd.

Enthoven, R. E. (1920-22). *The Tribes and Castes of
Bombay*. 3 volumes. Bombay: Government Central Press.

Epstein, R. Scarlett (1973). *South India: Yesterday,
Today and Tomorrow*. New York: Holmes and Meier Publishers, Inc.

Evans-Pritchard, E. E. (1940). *The Nuer*. Oxford: at
the Clarendon Press.

Fairservis, Walter A., Jr. (1971). *The Roots of Ancient India*. New York: Macmillan.

Fiske, Adele (1972). "Scheduled Caste Buddhist Organizations." In J. Michael Mahar, ed., *The Untouchables in Contemporary India*. Tucson: University of
Arizona Press.

Fortes, Meyer (1945). *The Dynamics of Clanship Among
the Tallensi*. London: Oxford University Press.

Fortes, Meyer (1945a). *The Web of Kinship Among the
Tallensi*. London: Oxford University Press.

Fortes, Meyer (1969). *Kinship and the Social Order*.
Chicago: Aldine Publishing Company.

Fox, Richard G. (1967). "Resiliency and Change in the
Indian Caste System: The Umar of U.P." *Journal of
Asian Studies* 26: 575-587.

Fox, Richard G. (1971). *Kin, Clan, Raja, and Rule*.
Berkeley, Los Angeles, and London: University of
California Press.

Fox, Richard G. (1973). "Pariah Capitalism and Tradition: Indian Merchants, Past and Present." In Milton
Singer, ed., *Entrepreneurship and Modernization of*

Occupational Cultures in South Asia. Duke University: Program in Comparative Studies in Southern Asia, Monograph Number 12, 16-36.

Franda, Marcus F. (1975). "India's Double Emergency Democracy." Three parts. *Fieldstaff Reports*. Hanover, New Hampshire: American Universities Field Staff.

Frankel, Francine R. (1971). *India's Green Revolution: Economic Gains and Political Costs*. Princeton, N.Y.: Princeton University Press.

Fried, Morton H. (1957). "The Classification of Corporate Unilineal Descent Groups." *Journal of the Royal Anthropological Institute* 87: 1-29.

Friedrich, Paul (1966). "Proto-Indo-European Kinship." *Ethnology* 5: 1-36.

Fuchs, Stephen (1965). *Rebellious Prophets*. New York: Asia Publishing House.

Fuller, C. J. (1976). *The Nayars Today*. London/New York: Cambridge University Press.

Fürer-Haimendorf, Christoph von (1967). "The Position of the Tribal Populations in Modern India." In Philip Mason, ed., *India and Ceylon: Unity and Diversity*. Institute of Race Relations. London, New York, Bombay: Oxford University Press, 182-222.

Galanter, Marc (1972). "The Abolition of Disabilities —Untouchability and the Law." In J. Michael Mahar, ed., *The Untouchables in Contemporary India*. Tucson: University of Arizona Press.

Ghurye, G. S. (1932). *Caste and Race in India*. London: Kegan Paul.

Ghurye, G. S. (1960). *After a Century and a Quarter*. Bombay: Popular Book Company.

Ghurye, G. S. (1961). *Caste, Class and Occupation*. Bombay: Popular Book Depot.

Gokhale, Jayashree (1977). "Dalit Panthers." Paper read at Twenty-ninth Annual Meeting of the Association for Asian Studies, New York City, March 27, 1977.

Gough, E. Kathleen (1955). "The Social Structure of a Tanjore Village." In E. R. Leach, ed., *Aspects of Caste in South India, Ceylon and North-West Pakistan*. Cambridge: Cambridge University Press.

Gough, E. Kathleen (1959). "The Nayars and the Definition of Marriage." *Journal of the Royal Anthropological Institute* 89: 23-34.

Gough, E. Kathleen (1960). "Caste in a Tanjore Village." In E. R. Leach, ed., *Aspects of Caste in South India, Ceylon and North-West Pakistan.* Cambridge: Cambridge University Press.

Gough, E. Kathleen (1974). "Indian Peasant Uprisings." *Economic and Political Weekly.* Special Number, August 1974, 1391-1412.

Gould, Harold A. (1958). "The Hindu Jajmani System: A Case of Economic Particularism." *Southwestern Journal of Anthropology* 14: 428-437.

Gould, Harold A. (1971). *Caste and Class: A Comparative View.* A McCaleb Module in Anthropology from the series Addison-Wesley Modular Publications. Reading, Mass.: Addison-Wesley.

Gould, Harold A. (1973). "Some Discussant Remarks Inspired by Robert Anderson's Comparison of the Careers of Homi Bhabha and Meghnad Saha." In Milton Singer, ed., *Entrepreneurship and Modernization of Occupational Cultures in South Asia.* Duke University: Program in Comparative Studies on Southern Asia. Monograph No. 12, 317-326.

Government of India (1972). *Statistical Abstract— India 1972.* New Delhi: Central Statistical Organisation, Department of Statistics, Ministry of Planning, Government of India. New Series, No. 19.

Hardgrave, Robert L., Jr. (1965). *The Dravidian Movement.* Bombay: Popular Prakashan.

Hardgrave, Robert L., Jr. (1968). "Caste Fission and Fusion." *Economic and Political Weekly,* Special Number, July 1968, 1065-1070.

Hardgrave, Robert L., Jr. (1969). *The Nadars of Tamilnad.* Berkeley and Los Angeles: University of California Press.

Harper, Edward B. (1964). "Ritual Pollution as an Integrator of Caste and Religion," *Religion in South Asia.* Seattle: University of Washington Press. 151-196.

Harper, Edward B. (1968a). "Social Consequences of an 'Unsuccessful' Low Caste Movement." In James Silverberg, ed., *Social Mobility in the Caste System in India. Comparative Studies in Society and History,* Supplement III. Hague and Paris: Mouton.

Harper, Edward B. (1968b). "A Comparative Analysis of Caste: The United States and India." In Milton

Singer and Bernard S. Cohn, eds., *Structure and Change in Indian Society*. Chicago: Aldine Publishing Company, 51-77.

Harris, Marvin (1971). *Culture, Man, and Nature*. New York: Thomas Y. Crowell Company.

Harrison, Selig (1960). *India, the Most Dangerous Decades*. Princeton: Princeton University Press.

Hitchcock, John (1956). "The Rajputs of Khalapur: A Study of Kinship, Social Stratification and Politics." Unpublished Ph.D. Dissertation, Cornell University.

Hitchcock, John (1960). "Surat Singh, Head Judge." In Joseph B. Casagrande, ed., *In the Company of Man*. New York: Harper and Brothers.

Hitchcock, John (1971). "Structural Paradox and Value Conflict in the Dominant Caste of a North Indian Village." In Mario D. Zamora, J. Michael Mahar, and Henry Orenstein, eds., *Themes in Culture*. Quezon City, Philippines: Kayumanggi Publishers.

Hitchcock, John (see Minturn below).

Hocart, A. M. (1950). *Caste*. London: Methuen and Company.

Hutton, J. H. (1963). *Caste in India*. (4th edition.) Oxford: Oxford University Press.

Ibbetson, Denzil Charles Jelf (1916). "Panjab Castes." Being a Reprint of the Chapter on "The Races, Castes . . . " In the *Census of the Punjab (1881)*. Lahore: Government Printing.

Isaacs, Harold R. (1965). *India's Ex-Untouchables*. Bombay: Asia Publishing House.

Isaacs, Harold R. (1972). "The Ex-Untouchables." In J. Michael Mahar, ed., *The Untouchables in Contemporary India*. Tucson: University of Arizona Press.

Johnson, Gordon (1973). *Provincial Politics and Indian Nationalism*. Cambridge: Cambridge University Press.

Joshi, P. C. (1974). "Land Reform and Agrarian Change in India and Pakistan Since 1947." *Journal of Peasant Studies* 1: 164-185, 327-362.

Karve, Irawati (1968). *Hindu Society—An Interpretation* (2nd edition). Budhwar, Poona: Deskmukh Prakashan.

Karve, Irawati and J. S. Randive (1965). *The Social Dynamics of a Growing Town and Its Surrounding Area*. Poona: Deccan College Research Institute.

Khare, R. S. (1970). *The Changing Brahmans*. Chicago: University of Chicago Press.

Khare, R. S. (1973). "One Hundred Years of Occupational Modernization Among KanyaKubja Brahmans: A Genealogical Reconstruction of Social Dynamics." In Milton Singer, ed., *Entrepreneurship and Modernization of Occupational Cultures in South Asia*. Duke University: Program in Comparative Studies on Southern Asia, Monograph No. 12.

Kolenda, Pauline Mahar (1963). "Toward a Model of the Hindu Jajmani System." *Human Organization* 22: 11-31.

Kolenda, Pauline Mahar (1964). "Religious Anxiety and Hindu Fate." *Journal of Asian Studies* 33: 71-81.

Kolenda, Pauline Mahar (1968). "Functional Relations of a Bhangi Cult." *Anthropologist* (University of Delhi). Special Volume II: 22-35.

Kothari, Rajni (1970). "Introduction: Caste in Indian Politics." In Rajni Kothari, ed., *Caste in Indian Politics*. New Delhi: Orient Longman Ltd.

Krader, Lawrence (1968). *Formation of the State*. Englewood Cliffs, New Jersey: Prentice-Hall, Inc.

Lambert, Richard D. (1963). *Workers, Factories and Social Change in India*. Princeton, New Jersey: Princeton University Press.

Laslett, Peter (1965). *The World We Have Lost*. London: Methuen and Co., Ltd.

Laslett, Peter, (ed.) (1972). *Household and Family in Past Time*. Cambridge: Cambridge University Press.

Leach, E. R. (1960). "Introduction: What Should We Mean by Caste?" In E. R. Leach, ed., *Aspects of Caste in South India, Ceylon, and North-West Pakistan*. Cambridge: Cambridge University Press.

Lewis, Oscar (1955). "Peasant Culture in India and Mexico: A Comparative Analysis." In McKim Marriott, ed., *Village India*. Chicago: University of Chicago Press, 145-170.

Lewis, Oscar (1958). *Village Life in Northern India*. Urbana: University of Illinois Press.

Lynch, Owen M. (1968). "The Politics of Untouchability —A Case from Agra, India." In Milton Singer and Bernard S. Cohn, eds., *Structure and Change in Indian Society*. Chicago: Aldine Publishing Company.

Lynch, Owen (1969). *The Politics of Untouchability*. New York: Columbia University Press.

Lynch, Owen M. (1974). "Political Mobilization and
Ethnicity among Adi-Dravidas in a Bombay Slum,"
Economic and Political Weekly IX (34) September 28,
1974, 1657-1668.

Mahar, Pauline Moller (1958). "Changing Caste Ideology
in a North Indian Village." *Journal of Social Issues*
14: 61-65.

Mahar, Pauline Moller (1959). "A Multiple Scaling
Technique for Caste Ranking." *Man in India* 39:
127-147.

Mahar, Pauline Moller (1960). "Changing Religious
Practices of an Untouchable Caste." *Economic Development and Cultural Change* 8: 279-287.

Maine, Sir Henry Sumner (1895). *Village-Communities in
the East and West.* London: John Murray.

Majumdar, D. N. (n.d.) *Races and Cultures of India*
Allhabad Kitabistan.

Malik, S. C. (1968). *Indian Civilization: The Forma-
tive Period.* Simla: Indian Institute of Advanced
Study.

Mandelbaum, David G. (1970). *Society in India.* Berkeley and Los Angeles: University of California Press.

Marriott, McKim (1960). "Caste Ranking and Community
Structure in Five Regions of India and Pakistan."
Poona: Deccan College Monograph.

Marriott, McKim (1968a). "Multiple Reference in Indian
Caste Systems." In James Silverberg, ed., *Social
Mobility in the Caste System in India. Comparative
Studies in Society and History,* Supplement III.
Hague and Paris: Mouton.

Marriott, McKim (1968b). "Caste Ranking and Food
Transactions: A Matrix Analysis." In Milton Singer
and Bernard S. Cohn, eds., *Structure and Change in
Indian Society.* Chicago: Aldine Publishing Company.

Marriott, McKim (1976). "Hindu Transactions: Diversity
Without Dualism." In Bruce Kapferer, ed., *Transac-
tion and Meaning.* Philadelphia: Institute for the
Study of Human Issues (ISHI). 109-142.

Marriott, McKim and Ronald B. Inden (1973). Caste Systems. *Encyclopaedia Britannica.* Vol. 3: 982-991.

Marriott, McKim and Ronald B. Inden (1977). "Toward an
Ethnosociology of South Asian Caste Systems." In
Kenneth A. David, ed., *The New Wind.* The Hague;
Mouton; Chicago: Aldine Publishers.

Marriott, McKim, Stanley A. Freed, and Ralph Nicholas (1967). "Hindu Caste Ranking." The Lewis Henry Morgan Lecture, The University of Rochester, Rochester, New York.

Mayer, Adrian C. (1958). "The Dominant Caste in a Region of Central India." *Southwestern Journal of Anthropology* 14:407-427.

Mayer, Adrian C. (1960). *Caste and Kinship in Central India*. Berkeley and Los Angeles: University of California Press.

McCrindle, J. W. (translator) (1877). Ancient India as described by Megasthenes and Arrian (being a translation of the fragments of the Indika of Megasthenes collected by Dr. Schwanbeck, and of the first part of the Indika of Arrian), Calcutta: Thacker, Spink & Co. Bombay: Thacker & Co. London: Trubner & Co.

Mencher, Joan P. (1972). "Continuity and Change in an Ex-Untouchable Community of South India." In J. Michael Mahar, ed., *The Untouchables in Contemporary India*. Tucson: University of Arizona Press.

Mencher, Joan P. (1974a). "The Caste System Upside Down, or the Not-so-Mysterious East," *Current Anthropology* 15: 469-478.

Mencher, Joan P. (1974b). "Group and Self-Identification: The View from the Bottom." *ICSSR* (Indian Council for Social Science) *Research Abstracts Quarterly* Volume III (nos. 2 & 3) 172-208.

Migdal, Joel S. (1974). *Peasants, Politics, and Revolution*, Princeton: Princeton University Press.

Miller, D. B. (1976). *From Hierarchy to Stratification: Changing Patterns of Social Inequality in a North Indian Village*. New York, New York: Oxford University Press.

Minturn, Leigh and John Hitchcock (1966). *The Rājpūts of Khalapur, India*. New York: John Wiley and Sons.

Montgomery, Edward (1972). "Kin Units, Local Resources, and Population Patterns." Paper read at the seventy-first meetings of the American Anthropological Association. Toronto.

Moore, Barrington, Jr. (1966). *Social Origins of Dictatorship and Democracy*. Boston: Beacon Press.

Morgan, Lewis Henry (1964). *Ancient Society*. Leslie A. White, ed. Cambridge: Belknap Press of Harvard University Press. (First published in 1877).

Muller, Max (1869). *Chips from a German Workshop*. Volume II. New York: Charles Scribner and Company.

Myrdal, Gunnar (1972). *Asian Drama*. (Abridged by Seth S. King). New York: Vintage Books, Random House.

Nair, Kusum (1969). *The Lonely Furrow*. Ann Arbor, Michigan: University of Michigan Press.

Natarajan, L. (1953). *Peasant Uprisings in India 1850-1900*. Bombay: People's Publishing House.

National Council of Applied Economic Research (1965). All India Rural Household Survey. Volume II: *Income, Investment and Saving*. New Delhi.

Nayar, V. K. S. (1966). "Communal Interest Groups in Kerala." In Donald Eugene Smith, ed., *South Asian Politics and Religion*. Princeton, New Jersey: Princeton University Press.

Neale, Walter C. (1957). "Reciprocity and Redistribution in the Indian Village: Sequel to Some Notable Discussions." In Karl Polanyi, Conrad M. Arensberg, and Harry W. Pearson, eds., *Trade and Market in the Early Empires*. New York: Free Press. 218-236.

Nesfield, John C. (1885). *Brief View of the Caste System of the North-Western Provinces and Oudh*. Allahabad: North-Western Provinces and Oudh Educational Department.

Nicholas, Ralph W. (1968). "Structure of Politics in the Villages of Southern Asia." In Milton Singer and Bernard S. Cohn, eds., *Structure and Change in Indian Society*. Chicago: Aldine Publishing Company.

Niehoff, Arthur (1959). *Factory Labor in India*. Milwaukee: Milwaukee Museum.

Opler, Morris E. (1956). "The Extensions of an Indian Village." *The Journal of Asian Studies* Volume 16, 5-10.

Orans, Martin (1965). *The Santal*. Detroit: Wayne State University Press.

Orenstein, Henry (1962). "Exploitation and Function in the Interpretation of Jajmani." *Southwestern Journal of Anthropology* 18: 302-315.

Orenstein, Henry (1963). "Caste and the Concept 'Maratha' in Maharashtra." *Eastern Anthropologist* 16: 1-9.

Orenstein, Henry (1965). *Gaon: Conflict and Cohesion in an Indian Village*. Princeton, New Jersey: Princeton University Press.

Orenstein, Henry (1970). Logical Congruence in Hindu Sacred Law: Another Interpretation. *Contributions to Indian Sociology*, New series, No. 4, 22-35.

Owens, Raymond (1973). "Peasant Entrepreneurs in a North Indian Industrial City." In Milton Singer, ed., *Entrepreneurship and Modernization of Occupational Cultures in South Asia*. Duke University: Program in Comparative Studies on Southern Asia, Monograph No. 12, 133-166.

Parsons, Talcott (1943). "The Kinship System of the Contemporary United States." *American Anthropologists* 45: 22-38.

Parsons, Talcott (1949). *The Structure of Social Action*. Glencoe, Illinois: The Free Press. (Originally published in 1937.)

Patel, Surendra J. (1952). *Agricultural Labourers in Modern India and Pakistan*. Bombay: Current Book House.

Pathak, R. C. (compiler and editor) (1946). *Bhargava's Standard Illustrated Dictionary of the Hindi Language*. Shree Ganga Pustakalaya, Gaighat, Banaras.

Patnaik, Nityananda (1960). Eight articles in Nirmal Kumar Bose, ed., *Data on Caste: Orissa*. Anthropological Survey of India, Calcutta, Memoir No. 7.

Patterson, M. L. P. (1968). "Chitpavan Brahman Family Histories: Sources for a Study of Social Structure and Social Change in Maharashtra." In Milton Singer and Bernard S. Cohn, eds., *Structure and Change in Indian Society*. Chicago: Aldine Publishers. 397-411.

Patwardhan, Sunanda (1973). *Change Among India's Harijans*. New Delhi: Orient Longman Ltd.

Panikkar, K. M. (1955). *Society at the Crossroads*. Bombay: Asia Publishing House.

Piggott, Stuart (1950). *Prehistoric India*. Baltimore, Maryland: Penguin Books.

Pike, Kenneth L. (1967). *Language in Relation to a Unified Theory of the Structure of Human Behavior*. The Hague: Mouton

Pitt-Rivers, Julian (1971). "On the Word 'Caste.'" In T. O. Beidelman, ed., *The Translation of Culture*. London: Tavistock Publications. 231-256.

Pocock, David (1955). "The Movement of Castes." *Man* 55: 71-72.

Pocock, David F. (1957). "Difference in East Africa: A Study of Caste and Religion in Modern Indian Society." *Southwestern Journal of Anthropology* 13: 289-300.

Pradhan, M. G. (1966). *The Political System of the Jats of Northern India.* London: Oxford University Press.

Radcliffe-Brown, A. R. (1935). "Patrilineal and Matrilineal Succession." The Iowa Law Review, Vol. XX. (Reprinted in *Structure and Function in Primitive Society.* Glencoe, Illinois: Free Press, 1952.)

Radcliffe-Brown, A. R. (1941). "The Study of Kinship Systems." *Journal of the Royal Anthropological Institute* 71: 1-18. Reprinted in *Structure and Function in Primitive Society.* Glencoe, Illinois: Free Press, 1952.

Radcliffe-Brown, A. R. (1950). "Introduction." In A. R. Radcliffe-Brown and Daryll Forde, eds., *African Systems of Kinship and Marriage.* International African Institute by Oxford University Press. 1-85.

Ram, Vangala J. (1971). "An Application of the Theory of Themes to Hindu Culture." In Mario D. Zamora, J. Michael Mahar, Henry Orenstein, eds., *Themes in Culture: Essays in Honor of Morris E. Opler.* Quezon City, Philippines: Kayumanggi Publishers, 307-325.

Rao, V. K. R. V. and P. B. Desai (1965). *Greater Delhi: A Study in Urbanization 1940-1957.* London: Asia Publishing House.

Retzlaff, Ralph H. (1962). *Village Government in India.* New York: Asia Publishing House.

Riesman, David (1950). *The Lonely Crowd.* New Haven: Yale University Press.

Rosenthal, Donald B. (1970). "Caste and Political Participation in Two Cities." In Rajni Kothari, ed., *Caste in Indian Politics.* New Delhi: Orient Longman Ltd., 340-370.

Rowe, William L. (1963). "Changing Rural Class Structure and the Jajmani System" *Human Organization* 22: 41-44.

Rowe, William L. (1968a). "Mobility in the Nineteenth Century Caste System." In Milton Singer and Bernard S. Cohn, eds., *Structure and Change in Indian Society.* Chicago: Aldine Publishing Company.

Rowe, William L. (1968b). "The New Cauhans: A Caste
Mobility Movement in North India." In James Silver-
berg, ed., *Social Mobility in the Caste System in
India*. Comparative Studies in Society and History,
Supplement III. Paris and Hague: Mouton.

Rowe, William L. (1973). "Caste, Kinship, and Associ-
ation in Urban India." In Aidan Southall, ed.,
Urban Anthropology. New York: Oxford University
Press, 211-249.

Roy, Ramashray (1970). "Caste and Political Recruit-
ment in Bihar." In Rajni Kothari, ed., *Caste in
Indian Politics*. New Delhi: Orient Longman Ltd.

Roy, Sarat Chandra (1934, 1937, 1938). "Caste, Race,
and Religion in India." *Man in India* XIV, No. 2;
XVII, No. 4; XVIII, Nos. 2 and 3.

Rudolph, Lloyd I. and Susanne Hoeber Rudolph (1967).
The Modernity of Tradition. Chicago and London:
University of Chicago Press.

Rudolph, Susanne Hoeber and Lloyd I. Rudolph (1972).
Education and Politics in India. Cambridge: Harvard
University Press.

Sahlins, Marshall D. (1968). *Tribesmen*. Englewood
Cliffs, New Jersey: Prentice-Hall, Inc.

Sastri, K. A. Nilakanta (1963). *Development of Religion in South India*. Bombay: Orient Longman Ltd.

Schneider, David M. and Calvert B. Cottrell (1975).
The American Kin Universe: A Genealogical Study.
The University of Chicago Studies in Anthropology
Series in Social, Cultural, and Linguistic Anthro-
pology, No. 3.

Schwartzberg, Joseph E. *Occupational Structure and
Level of Economic Development in India: A Regional
Analysis*. Census of India 1961 Monograph Series,
Monograph No. 4.

Service, Elman R. (1975). *Origins of the State and
Civilization: the Process of Cultural Evolution*.
New York: W. W. Norton and Company, Inc.

Shah, A. M. (1964). "Political System in Eighteenth
Century Gujarat." *Enquiry* 1: 33-95.

Sharma, K. N. (1969). "Resource Networks and Resource
Groups in the Social Structure." *Eastern Anthropologist* 22: 13-27.

Shils, Edward (1960). *The Indian Intellectual Between
Tradition and Modernity: The Indian Situation*. The
Hague: Mouton.

Silverberg, James, ed., (1968). *Social Mobility in the Caste System in India*. Comparative Studies in Society and History, Supplement III. Hague and Paris: Mouton.

Singer, Milton (1961). "Review of Max Weber, The Religion of India." *American Anthropologist* 63: 143-151.

Singer, Milton (1972). *When a Great Tradition Modernizes*. New York, Washington, London: Praeger Publishers.

Singer, Milton (1973). "Introduction: The Modernization of Occupational Cultures in South Asia." In Milton Singer, ed., *Entrepreneurship and Modernization of Occupational Cultures in South Asia*. Duke University, Program of Comparative Studies in Southern Asia, Monograph Number 12, 1-15.

Singh, Mohinder (1947). *The Depressed Classes*. Bombay: Hind Kitabs Ltd., Publishers.

Singh, Kushwant (1965). "The Nagas." In Guy Wint, ed., *Asia: A Handbook*. London: Anthony Blond, 466-470.

Singh, Vijai P. (1976). *Caste, Class, and Democracy*. Cambridge, Massachusetts: Schenkman Publishing Company.

Sinha, Surajit (1965). "Tribe-Caste and Tribe-Peasant Continua in Central India." *Man in India* 45: 57-83.

Sisson, Richard (1970). "Caste and Political Factions in Rajasthan." In Rajni Kothari, ed., *Caste in Indian Politics*. New Delhi: Orient Longman Ltd.

Smith, Donald Eugene (1963). *India as a Secular State*. Princeton, New Jersey: Princeton University Press.

Spear, Percival (1962). *India: A Modern History*. Ann Arbor: University of Michigan Press.

Srinivas, M. N. (1952). *Religion and Society Among the Coorgs of South India*. London: Oxford University Press.

Srinivas, M. N. (1955). "The Social System of a Mysore Village." In McKim Marriott, ed., *Village India*. Chicago: University of Chicago Press.

Srinivas, M. N. (1959). "The Dominant Caste in Rampura." *American Anthropologist* 61: 1-16.

Srinivas, M. N. (1962). "Caste in Modern India." In M. N. Srinivas, *Caste in Modern India and Other Essays*. London: Asia Publishing House (originally published in *Journal of Asian Studies*, 1957, 16: 529-548).

Srinivas, M. N. (1968). "Mobility of the Caste System." In Milton Singer and Bernard S. Cohn, eds., *Structure and Change in Indian Society*. Chicago: Aldine Publishers.

Srinivas, M. N. (1969). *Social Change in Modern India*. Berkeley and Los Angeles: University of California Press.

Srivastava, Ram P. (1966). "Tribe-Caste Mobility in India and the Case of the Kumaon Bhotias." In Christoph von Fürer-Haimendorf, eds., Thurston, F. and K. Rangachari (1909). *Caste and Kin in Nepal, India, and Ceylon*. Bombay: Asia Publishing House, 161-212.

Stein, Burton (1968). "Social Mobility and Medieval South Indian Hindu Sects." In James Silverberg, ed., *Social Mobility in the Caste System in India. Comparative Studies in Society and History*, Supplement III. Paris and Hague: Mouton.

Stein, Burton (1969). "Integration of the Agrarian System of South India." In Robert Eric Frykenberg, ed., *Land Control and Social Structure in Indian History*. Madison, Milwaukee, and London: University of Wisconsin Press.

Stevenson, H. N. C. (1954). "Status Evaluation in the Hindu Caste System" *Journal of the Royal Anthropological Institute* 4: 45-65.

Thurston, F. and Rangachari, K. (1909). *Castes and Tribes of Southern India*. 7 volumes. Madras: Government Press.

Toye, J. F. (1977). "Economic Trends and Policies in India During the Emergency." *World Development* 5: 303-316.

Travancore Devaswom Manual, Travancore Devaswom Board 1955.

Tyler, Stephen A. (1973). *India: An Anthropological Perspective*. Pacific Palisades, California: Goodyear Publishing Company.

Ullrich, Helen E., ed., (1975). *Competition and Modernization in South Asia*. New Delhi: Abhinav.

Vatuk, Sylvia (1972). *Kinship and Urbanization: White Collar Migrants in North India*. Berkeley, London, and Los Angeles: University of California Press.

Vidyarthi, P. P. (1972). "Tribal Ethnography in India." In *A Survey of Research in Sociology and Social Anthropology*. Bombay: Popular Prakashan, 31-133.

Wasson, R. Gordon (1968). *Soma: Divine Mushroom of Immortality*. Italy: Harcourt Brace Jovanovich, Inc.

Weber, Max (1958). *The Religion of India*. Glencoe, Illinois: The Free Press. (Originally published in German in 1920-21.)

White, L. A. (1939). "A Problem in Kinship Terminology." *American Anthropologist* 16: 569-570.

Whyte, William H., Jr. (1956). *The Organization Man*. New York: Simon & Schuster.

Wiebe, Paul D. (1975). *Social Life in an Indian Slum*. Delhi/Bombay: Vikas Publishing House.

Williams, Robin M., Jr. (1951). *American Society*. New York: Alfred Knopf.

Wiser, William H. (1958). *The Hindu Jajmani System*. Lucknow: Lucknow Publishing House. (Originally published in 1936.)

Wiser, William and Charlotte Wiser (1971). *Behind Mud Walls 1930-1960: With a Sequel: The Village in 1970*. Berkeley and Los Angeles: University of California Press. (*Behind Mud Walls* originally published in 1930.)

Wolf, Eric R. (1966). *Peasants*. Englewood Cliffs, New Jersey: Prentice-Hall, Inc.

Yalman, Nur (1963). "On the Purity of Women in the Castes of Ceylon and Malabar." *Journal of the Royal Anthropological Institute* 3(part 1): 25-58.

Yalman, Nur (1967). *Under the Bo Tree*. Berkeley: University of California Press.

Zelliott, Eleanor (1966). "Buddhism and Politics in Maharashtra." In Donald Eugene Smith, ed., *South Asian Politics and Religion*. Princeton, New Jersey: Princeton University Press.

Zelliot, Eleanor (1970). "Learning the Use of Political Means: The Mahars of Maharashtra." In Rajni Kothari, ed., *Caste in Indian Politics*. Delhi: Orient Longman Ltd.

Zelliot, Eleanor (1972). "Gandhi and Ambedkar—A Study in Leadership." In J. Michael Mahar, ed., *The Untouchables in Contemporary India*. Tucson: University of Arizona Press.

Zimmer, Heinrich (1960). *Philosophies of India*. New York: Meridian Books. (Originally published in 1951.)

Subject Index

Authors Index

Index of Caste and Tribe Names